of America Chamberlain Association

Report of Annual Meetings Held in Boston, Massachuseltt,

September 12, 1906 and August 1, 1907

of America Chamberlain Association

Report of Annual Meetings Held in Boston, Massachuseltt, September 12, 1906 and August 1, 1907

ISBN/EAN: 9783744734929

Printed in Europe, USA, Canada, Australia, Japan

Cover: Foto ©ninafisch / pixelio.de

More available books at **www.hansebooks.com**

Hon. George Earle Chamberlain
Governor of Oregon, 1903 --

THE
CHAMBERLAIN ASSOCIATION
OF AMERICA

REPORT OF ANNUAL MEETINGS HELD IN BOSTON, MASSA-
CHUSETTS, SEPTEMBER, 12, 1906, AND AUGUST 1, 1907

WITH

MEMORIAL AND BIOGRAPHICAL SKETCHES OF MEMBERS OF THE
ASSOCIATION

FOUR GENERATIONS OF THE DESCENDANTS OF HENRY CHAMBERLIN OF
HINGHAM, ENGLAND, AND HINGHAM, MASSACHUSETTS

TRANSCRIPTS FROM THE PARISH REGISTERS OF HINGHAM, ENGLAND,

AND OTHER

PAPERS CONCERNING THE CHAMBERLAIN FAMILY IN ENGLAND AND
AMERICA

NEW YORK
THE GRAFTON PRESS
Issued from the press, June, 1908

The committee on publication regrets exceedingly the delay in the issuing of this report. The Executive Committee hopes that the report for 1908 will be sent to the members in less than twelve months.

CHAMBERLAIN ASSOCIATION OF AMERICA

ANNUAL MEETING OF 1906

ON September 12, 1906, the Association held its annual gathering (the ninth in its history) at the Parker House, Boston.

The business meeting was called to order at 2:45 by the President, General Joshua L. Chamberlain, and the routine business was disposed of.

The report of the Genealogical Committee led to a lengthy and animated discussion, the question at issue being, "Shall the Genealogical Bureau be maintained as a separate organization, or shall it be consolidated with the Genealogical Committee?" Finally a vote was passed referring the matter to the President and Executive Committee with full power to decide.

A biographical sketch of the late John Frederick Chamberlin of New York was read.

The business meeting adjourned at five o'clock, and at six the members assembled for dinner. When the coffee was served the President delivered a brief address,—he had been re-elected in spite of his earnestly expressed desire that the reins of government be placed in other hands. Addresses were delivered, also, by Judge Forbes and General Samuel E. Chamberlain. Dr. George M. Chamberlin of Chicago made a stirring speech, followed in much the same vein by Dr. E. W. Chamberlain of New York.

A biographical sketch of Jacob Chester Chamberlin, of New York, which had been prepared by Rev. L. T. Chamberlain, D. D., of New York, was read by Mr. Asa Chamberlin, of Jamaica Plain.

The post-prandial exercises were enlivened by vocal and instrumental selections by Miss Ella M. Chamberlain, Cambridge, and Miss Bertha C. Chamberlain, Norwood.

The finale was the singing of "America" by the entire assembly.

MONTAGUE CHAMBERLAIN,
Recording Secretary.

REPORT OF THE CORRESPONDING SECRETARY

One of the gratifying features we report to-day, is a large accession of members, chiefly from the Chamberlain Reunion Association formed in August, 1905, —a grouping of the descendants of Benjamin Chamberlain, who died near Sparta, N. J., in 1816. In the list of deaths recorded, all will regret to see the name of one of our distinguished Vice-Presidents, Col. H. H. Adams, of New York City, whose portrait and biography were included in our Annual Report for 1903. Our sympathies have been called forth by the long, painful illness of Mr. Eugene G. Chamberlin of Chicago, so beautifully borne, while tenderly nursed by his faithful wife. The death of the prominent New York banker, Mr. John F. Chamberlin, of Summit, N. J., has been reported by his brother, Mr. Emerson Chamberlin. We are glad to welcome the daughter of Mrs. Amy Chamberlain Shanks to fill the vacancy caused by her mother's passing away last year. Death claimed Mr. James I. Chamberlain as a victim of pneumonia in June. Both he and his wife were with us at our fifth annual meeting. Mrs. Judge Furst of Bellefonte, Pa., has been doubly bereaved by the death of this brother, followed later by that of her distinguished husband, a prominent lawyer and judge. Miss Sarah Chamberlain, of Salem, Mass., has lost her only brother, Mr. Edward Watts Chamberlain, of Louisville, Ky. The first money received in the Chamberlain treasury came from him and his son. Mrs. J. S. Brown of La Grange, Ind., is deeply bereaved by the sudden death of her excellent husband. She is the sister of our wonderful traveller, Capt. Orville T. Chamberlain.

Photographs of two Vice-Presidents have been received,—Mr. Richard H. Chamberlain, of Oakland, Cal., and Mr. W. W. Chamberlaine, of Norfolk, Va. A photograph of Mr. W. N. Chamberlin, of New Carlisle, Ohio, has been received. We sympathize with him in the loss of his beloved wife, Mrs. Sarah Jane Osborn Chamberlin, in March, 1906. We congratulate him upon reaching his eighty-fourth birthday, May 28th. You will make his acquaintance through his picture in this Report.

If "history is perennially interesting," personal records are much more so, and may serve as a stimulus to the younger generation, for we have been brought through the camera and pen into closer acquaintance with some of our officers and members by our biennial report, which seemed to give much pleasure and satisfaction to our distant members. Their patience had been somewhat taxed by the great printers' strike all over the country delaying its completion, but the Chairman of the Committee on History, with characteristic energy, faithfully pressed the work to completion, and all feel well rewarded for the delay. Some, in these sketches, have taken us into their inner life, and told us of their boyish ambitions and later achievements. Special thanks are due Gen. Joshua L. Chamberlain, President McKendree H. Chamberlin, Dr. E. E. Strong, and Mrs. John C. Ordway, for so kindly loaning us plates for the illustrations.

The question for discussion to-day is, in what form and way shall we begin the publishing of our genealogy? The decision rests with the Association. Our Chamberlain horizon was considerably broadened last June, when visiting Dr. and Mrs. George M. Chamberlin in their delightful home on Drexel Boulevard, Chicago. The hospitable doctor telephoned to all parts of Greater Chicago, asking our Chamberlain members to call and learn about their "eastern cousins." Many responded, coming even in a drenching rain from twelve miles out; and we found western hospitality was not narrowed to the definition in the dictionary.

MR. WALTER N. CHAMBERLIN

The officers of this Association have much cause for gratitude that the majority of the members have so loyally supported and encouraged them in this labor of love; and if all of you will continue to exercise patience and forbearance, they, or their successors, may be able to carry out in the future all of your plans and wishes. Thanking you for the many expressions of kindness in the past,

Faithfully submitted,
ABBIE MELLEN CHAMBERLAIN.

CAMBRIDGE, MASS., 1906.

REPORT OF THE TREASURER

In account with the Chamberlain Association

FROM SEPTEMBER 13, 1905, TO SEPTEMBER 12, 1906

1905.	DR.	
Sept. 8.	Balance on hand,	$300.04
	Yearly fees,	219.00
	New members,	33.00
	Sale of reports,	17.45
		$569.49

1905.	CR.	
Sept. 13.	Paid Parker House, use of the Crystal Room during annual meeting.	$10.00
Oct. 13.	Paid Mr. George W. Chamberlain, Bureau Secretary,	75.00
Dec. 11.	Suffolk Engraving Co., Boston,	5.82
1906.		
April 17.	Smith & Sale, printing 550 annual reports (1904–5),	161.47
	Express,	1.70
	Collection on checks,	.64
	Paper, envelopes, postage,	44.26
	Frank Wood, printing notices of annual meeting, 1906,	3.00
		$301.89
Sept. 12.	Balance in hands of Assistant Treasurer,	267.60
		$569.49

SOPHIA A. CHAMBERLAIN CASWELL,
Assistant Treasurer.

ANNUAL MEETING OF 1907

The tenth annual meeting of the Association, which was held at the Parker House, Boston, on the first day of August, 1907, was characterized by a feeling of comradeship such as few of these reunions have attained. The majority of those present, widely separated as are their home towns, had met so frequently at these gatherings that they were no longer strangers, and those who were making their first appearance soon became infected with the general good fellowship about them.

The Executive Committee met at ten o'clock, and before their deliberations were ended the first comers were announced, and by noon a goodly number had assembled, and were formally welcomed by the President, Gen. Joshua L. Chamberlain, assisted by Vice-President Samuel E. Chamberlain and Mrs. Samuel E. Chamberlain.

After an hour spent in greeting old friends and forming new acquaintances the company was served with luncheon in the Crystal Room, where the Clan Chamberlain have gathered yearly since the Association was organized.

The good things provided by mine host having been disposed of, the routine business,—reading of the reports from Secretary and Treasurer and from Committees,—was taken up, sandwiched between divers entertaining talks and delightful music.

The guests of honor were Ex-Governor and Mrs. Chamberlain of Connecticut. Mr. Pierson Chamberlain, President of the New Jersey Chamberlain Reunion Association, and Mr. John Chase, President of the Chase-Chace Family Association, all of whom made interesting addresses. Mr. Chase complimented the Chamberlain Association on its large membership and its vigor and its loyalty to the family traditions, and invited the Association to send a representative to the next year's annual gathering of the Chase-Chace families.

Gen. Samuel E. Chamberlain added to the festivity by relating a number of amusing stories in his inimitable way.

The Treasurer assured the meeting that the finances were in sound condition, as we had $560.70 in the Quincy Savings Bank as well as $281.44 in the custody of the Assistant Treasurer.

The Committee on English Ancestry reported that they had prepared for publication a paper on Henry Chamberlin of Hingham, Mass., and Hingham, England.

A vote was passed, "that we accept, with thanks to Dr. George M. Chamberlin, of Chicago, the translation of the epitaph on the tomb of Dr. Hugo Chamberlen, in Westminster Abbey."

Telegrams were received from Prof. Paul Mellen Chamberlain and from

George M. Chamberlin, M.D.

Dr. George M. Chamberlin, both of Chicago, and replies were drafted and despatched as the exercises proceeded.

A motion was introduced to raise the admission fee to $2.00 and the annual dues to $2.00. A rather lively debate ensued, and the majority of the speakers being opposed to the change, the motion was withdrawn.

Colonel Harding, of New York, told, in an entertaining way, of his search for the ancestry of his wife, who was a Chamberlain. His address was filled with valuable suggestions for the prosecution of genealogical research. Mrs. Harding also made a brief address, as did Mr. Eugene Chamberlin, Mrs. Fellows and Mr. Emerson Chamberlin, all of New York; Mrs. Platt, of Englewood, N. J.; Mr. Edward Chamberlain, of San Antonio, Tex.; and Messrs. Albert and Augustus Chamberlin (twins), of North Abington, Mass. Music was rendered by Mrs. Davis, Mrs. Perry, Miss Lilla A. Chamberlin and Miss Ella Chamberlain.

A poem, written for this occasion by Mrs. Smiley of Holyoke, Mass., had been printed by Mr. Asa Chamberlin of Jamaica Plain, and copies were distributed to the guests, who sang it to the tune of "Auld Lang Syne."

Then the meeting adjourned.

MONTAGUE CHAMBERLAIN,
Recording Secretary.

REPORT OF THE CORRESPONDING SECRETARY

To-day we have met to celebrate the tenth anniversary of our Association. One of our pleasant privileges at our annual gatherings is to give a personal greeting to distant members. We are glad to clasp them by the hand, look in their faces and say, "welcome." Last year (1906) the banquet in the eve closed an all-day's business session of the Executive Committee and the Association. The Crystal Room was beautiful; the dinner-tables were adorned with a profusion of lovely flowers, chiefly from the estate of Judge William T. Forbes of Worcester, and the arches behind the President's chair were draped with the large fine flag which keeps the memory of its giver, the late Col. H. H. Adams, of New York City, fresh in our thoughts. Speeches and excellent music and the best dinner the Parker House has ever served the Association, united to make the occasion most enjoyable. The President was very happy in introducing the speakers and musicians. The special feature of interest was an able historic paper by Judge William T. Forbes, showing careful research in his subject, "Services of Massachusetts Chamberlains in the French and Indian Wars, as shown by the State Archives, with some account of the captives in Canada, and their descendants." This led to interesting remarks from Mr. Montague Chamberlain, of Boston, a well-known friend of the Indians, and to bright, pleasing addresses by Dr. George M. Chamberlin, of Chicago, and Mr. Edwin Chamberlin, of New York City. Brigadier-General Samuel E. Chamberlain, of Barre Plains, closed with some of his delightful reminiscences.

CHAMBERLAIN ASSOCIATION OF AMERICA

There have been seventeen accessions to the Association the past year, and four deaths have been reported,—Hon. D. H. Chamberlain, formerly Governor of South Carolina, a prominent man and a Vice-President of this Association; Hon. Henry Chamberlain, a pioneer in the State of Michigan; Mr. Jacob A. Chamberlain, of Warwick, N. Y., a well-known business man in New York City, and Miss Henrietta Maria Chamberlaine, of Baltimore, Md., the compiler of that interesting booklet, "Notes on the Maryland Chamberlaines." We thank the friends who sent notices and newspaper clippings relating to these members, as they are invaluable in the preliminary work of preparing biographical sketches. We acknowledge the receipt of photographs from Governor Chamberlain, of Oregon, Mr. Raymond Chamberlain and Mr. Archie S. Chamberlain, both of Brooklyn, N. Y., and the loan of several photographs for use in the coming Report. We have been favored with a fine large picture of the house of Dr. George M. Chamberlin, and another of Drexel Boulevard, on which it is located in Chicago; also a photograph of the hospitable home of General and Mrs. Samuel E. Chamberlain, of Barre Plains, Mass. Mr. Warren Chamberlain, of Honolulu, one of our most loyal and interested members, has sent a large illustrated number of a Honolulu newspaper, showing the remarkable growth of Hawaii for the past fifty years; also a catalogue of Oahu College, with a history of its foundation, and a photograph and brief sketch of his ancestor, Levi Chamberlain, who sailed April 27, 1823, under the A. B. C. F. M., as a missionary to the Hawaiian Islands. A copy of the Telugu Bible Dictionary by Jacob Chamberlain, M. D., D. D., of Coonoor, India, has been received; also a picture of himself with his interpreter, J. J. Rayappa, working in his library; and a leaflet with the story of twelve Brahmins. Mr. Raymond Chamberlain has sent a Report of the Brooklyn Teachers' Association for 1906. A copy of the Catalogue of McKendree College at Lebanon, Ill., comes from its President. Capt. Orville T. Chamberlain is still circling the globe, but has not forgotten to send us notes from Honolulu, and some data from California. Miss Ella Chamberlain, our popular whistler, has turned her attention partially to Art, and is making for her friends very good copies of the favorite coat of arms of the Chamberlain family. Miss Isabella S. Chamberlin, of Washington, D. C., has sent interesting Revolutionary data. Two of our members have contributed to the department of English history. Dr. J. W. Chamberlin, of St. Paul, Minn., has sent two plates, which enable us to reproduce in this Report the portrait of Dr. Hugh Chamberlen, of London, England, and his cenotaph in Westminster Abbey. Dr. George M. Chamberlin has furnished a translation of the epitaph. Our distant member, Mrs. S. C. Eccleston, who has experienced such phenomenal success in organizing Kindergartens in Buenos Ayres and throughout the Argentine Republic, has purchased a school building, intending to establish a Normal School for the training of her assistants. Mrs. Anna E. Smiley, who wrote an "Old Home Week" song for us to sing to the tune of "Auld Lang Syne" at our annual meeting, has gone to Old Hadley to reside. Mr. Townshend, in charge of our banquets at the Parker House, was highly complimented

last year for the fine dinner served and courteous treatment received. We are happy to credit all of our members for their kindly interest and contributions.

Ten years ago when, through the courtesy of Dr. E. E. Strong, our first two meetings were held in the famous room 13 of the old Congregational House, Boston (13 persons in room 13, with no foreboding of evil), and he moved that we form a Chamberlain Association, few thought that it would extend beyond New England, although encouraged by Mr. Henry A. May, Secretary of the Roxbury Military Historical Society, who had written that, in gathering historical and genealogical data for a history, he had visited one hundred and eighty towns and cities, and had found so many bearing the name Chamberlain, that he believed the family was one of the largest in the United States. Later he wrote that in preparing a list of four thousand names of Revolutionary soldiers in New England for the Sons of the American Revolution in order to place markers on their graves, he had found Chamberlain records in two-thirds of the places which he had visited, and thought there were more soldiers of that name than of any other in the records of New England. This was a tribute to Chamberlain patriotism, and an inspiration to the formation of this Association. Our first money came from Kentucky, and later applications for membership came from the middle and the extreme western states. Evidently our scope and name must be enlarged. We are now known as the Chamberlain Association of America, and members are found in thirty-nine different states, territories and countries. As Boston is the headquarters, Massachusetts ranks the highest, with ninety-three members. New York comes next with forty-one names, New Jersey and Illinois twenty-two each, Pennsylvania twenty, Michigan fifteen, Connecticut fourteen, Ohio thirteen, Vermont and Maine each eight, New Hampshire, Indiana, and Iowa seven each, Minnesota six, and the State of Washington and the District of Columbia five each. Two of our members reside in the Hawaiian Islands, one at Manila, one in India, one in the Argentine Republic, and one in England. There has been a gradual but steady increase in our membership, although deaths have been reported each year. During ten years there have been forty-three deaths.

Due credit has been given to the noble work of Mr. Jacob Chester Chamberlain in helping to found the Genealogical Bureau, and to trace his own branch; and reference has been made to Dr. L. T. Chamberlain's support of the work in English ancestry. Judge Mellen Chamberlain left valuable historical and genealogical data relating to our family in the "Chamberlain Alcove" of the Boston Public Library. About forty members of various patriotic societies have joined this organization, with their lines traced for five or more generations—a valuable acquisition to the records of our Association. We have representatives from three societies, formed by three different branches of our large family—the Pennsylvania society, descendants of Wright Chamberlain of the Richard of Braintree branch; the society in western New York, descendants of Numian and Jeremiah Chamberlain, who settled near Gettysburg, Pa., about 1742 (it is supposed), but removed to the neighbourhood of Niles in New York in 1807;

and the Chamberlain Reunion Association of New Jersey, descendants of Benjamin Chamberlain, who, previous to 1767, journeyed from Connecticut to Sussex County, N. J., where he died in 1816. All of these facts only whet the edge of interest.

This Association began without one cent in the treasury, and has always conducted its business on a cash basis. No officer has received any compensation, and no outstanding debts have been incurred. The money saved from the yearly membership fees, including the five life memberships (twenty-five dollars each), has been deposited in a Savings Bank (usually at four per cent interest) until it has reached the present amount of $560.70, besides the current funds in the hands of the Assistant Treasurer. This Association not only has a fine record for business integrity, but also its Annual Report is sought for by the State and the leading city libraries of this country, and a copy of each issue is sent to the "Keeper of the Library of the British Museum, London, England." We have much cause for encouragement, since a special committee of the Executive Board plans to begin the publication of our genealogy by an account of the first immigrant to New England, Henry Chamberlin, of Hingham, and his descendants, to be followed (it is hoped) by that of other branches. By this, we trust, new life and inspiration will be awakened in our Association. If each member (who has not already done so) will sit down to-morrow and write out his or her family line in the ascending scale as far as possible, it may save much time, labor, and expense in publishing the Chamberlain records.

We believe the Chamberlain history is rich and strong, and many noble types of manhood and womanhood are to be found in it. The past is vibrant with life; we only need time and co-operation to develop this history. We close with thanks to our noble Vice-Presidents and distant members, for their many kindly words and letters of sympathy, as well as to our more recent members for their active interest in this Association.

Sincerely submitted,
ANNIE MELLEN CHAMBERLAIN.

CAMBRIDGE, MASS., August 1, 1907.

Special thanks are due for two printed genealogical records, which have arrived since this report was written. A portion of Colonel Harding's pamphlet, received in December, will be reprinted in this Report. In March, Mr. Pierson Chamberlain, President of the Chamberlain Reunion Association of New Jersey, sent a book printed for the members of that society and entitled, *A Genealogical Record of the Descendants of Benjamin Chamberlain of Sussex County, New Jersey*, by Rev. A. J. Fretz, of Milton, N. J. Benjamin Chamberlain,—born in Connecticut in 1746, died in New Jersey in 1816, farmer, shoemaker, and Revolutionary soldier,—is highly honored by the large band of his descendants who meet yearly to bind more closely the ties of kinship. Their names and life-histories and, in many instances, their faces look out from these pages to add to our acquaintance. The introduction is written by Mr. Raymond Chamberlain, of Brooklyn, New York.

ANNUAL MEETING OF 1907

REPORT OF THE TREASURER

In account with the Chamberlain Association

FROM SEPTEMBER 12, 1906, TO AUGUST 1, 1907

1906.		DR.	
Sept. 12.		Balance on hand,	$267.60
		Yearly fees,	228.00
		New members,	16.00
		Exchange on checks,	.20
		Sale of reports,	10.20
			522.00
1906.		CR.	
Sept. 12.		Expenses of annual meeting—express, decorations, etc.,	$4.00
1907.			
Jan.		Paid express on receipts for annual dues,	.15
		Paid Frank Wood, printing receipts for annual dues,	3.00
July	9.	Paid Frank Wood, printing notices of meeting, 1907,	2.75
		Collection on checks,	.60
		Paper, envelopes, postage,	30.06
			$40.56
1906.			
Oct.	1.	Deposited in Quincy Savings Bank,	$200.00
1907.			
Aug.	1.	Balance in hands of Assistant Treasurer,	281.44
			$522.00
		Total sum in Quincy Savings Bank,	$560.70

SOPHIA A. CHAMBERLAIN CASWELL,
Assistant Treasurer.

IN MEMORIAM

JACOB CHESTER CHAMBERLAIN

By Rev. Leander T. Chamberlain, D. D.

The announcement, "Died in New York, July 28, 1905, of acute pneumonia, Jacob Chester Chamberlain, aged forty-five," carried special sorrow to many hearts in this and other lands. It was the end, as unexpected as appalling, of a life distinguished by achievement and radiant with promise. To wife and child the event came as when earthquake and tempest smite suddenly, or the unsuspected rock sends to instant destruction the staunch, swift ship. To every beholder it was like the falling of a fatal bolt from a clear, blue sky. The superbest of physical constitutions succumbed to an attack which nothing mortal could withstand. The strong man armed was overborne by a foe both resistless and relentless. Love watched and prayed, and skill wrought, and utmost rescources were enlisted; but the progress of disease was not even hindered. Again might it be said, as of old in Israel, "He was swifter than an eagle, he was stronger than a lion. How are the mighty fallen in the midst of the battle."

To more than one lover of the departed came Milton's incomparable lament:—

"For Lycidas is dead, dead ere his prime.
Young Lycidas, and hath not left his peer.
*   *   *   *   *   *   *
And oh the heavy change, now thou art gone,
Now thou art gone and never must return.

Mr. Chamberlain was of honorable lineage. His first progenitor in this country was that William Chamberlain of England who was living in Woburn, Mass., in 1648, one of the founders of Billerica in 1653, and dying there in 1706. His birth was in India, July 3, 1860,—eldest son of Jacob Chamberlain, M. D., D. D., the veteran missionary of the Reformed Church, now in the forty-seventh year of his illustrious service. On his mother's side—Charlotte (Birge) Chamberlain—he came of stock equally worthy,—gentleness and sweetness joined with heroic courage.

When twelve years old, he was sent to this country to be educated. At the age of eighteen he entered Rutgers College, New Brunswick, N. J., where he was graduated with honor in 1882. Naturally appreciative of science, both pure and applied, he chose a year's post-graduate course in chemistry, and then entered upon his career as an electrician. From the first, he was distinguished by the breadth of his researches. The laws and forces of electricity were to him far more

Mr. Jacob Chester Chamberlain

than mere materials for commercial, industrial exploitation. In them he discovered the perfection of harmony, the illustration of sovereign order. For him the harmony was akin to music, and the order was like the rythm of the seasons and the tides. To suggestions coming from those laws and forces he listened as to oracles inspired. He honored their demands as being, in fact, the wise decrees of God. From even his professional occupation came motive for his personal character. He realized that Science was wholly veracious, and that Nature always kept faith. Therefore he himself the more loved truth and fashioned his soul in honor's likeness. In the realm of his fond researches, he soared on exultant, tireless wing at the same time that he made his discoveries practical and coined them into money values.

The record of his work and progress is full of interest; assistant in Mr. Edison's laboratory; active operator in the first Edison electric light station in Pearl Street, New York City; suggester, in that service, of important electrical improvements; engineer and superintendent of construction in the Sawyer-Mann Electric Company; engineer of the Julien Traction Company, in their introduction of storage-battery cars; patentee of numerous devices for perfecting the storage-battery system for railway works; successful developer of the construction and equipment of electric launches; and general manager of the Automatic Refrigerating Company, whose electrical refrigerating system he brought to a satisfactory issue. Withal, an unwearied worker, a devoted explorer, a constant inventor, a successful business manager, an able financier.

Early in his professional career, Mr. Chamberlain was honored with the degree of Master of Science. He was one of the early members of the American Institute of Electrical Engineers; Chairman of House Committee in the old Electric Club; member of the Colonial Club; the Marine Field Club; the Grolier Club; and the Engineers' Club. While he was active in all these organizations, it was in the Grolier Club and the Engineers' Club that his greatest interest centered. In them all he was esteemed not only for his faithful services, but also for his personal worth and charm. His death called forth honoring tributes from various sources; among others, from the *Electrical World and Engineer;* the Automatic Refrigerating Company; the Rutgers Chapter of the Delta Upsilon Fraternity; and the New England Historic Genealogical Society.

On June 12, 1895, Mr. Chamberlain married Anna Mary Irwin, daughter of William P. Irwin, Esq., of Albany, N. Y. The result was a charming realization of the words of Dr. Jowett, the famous Master of Balliol: "Marriage is the greatest event of life. It is the best and most lasting thing. It is heaven upon earth to live together in perfect amity and disinterestedness and unselfishness, in the service of God and man, until our life is over." Long ago Izaak Walton described the felicity of that home, when he wrote of holy George Herbert and his wife Jane: "The eternal Lover of mankind made them happy in each other's mutual and equal affections; indeed, so happy that there never was any opposition betwixt them, unless it were a contest which should most incline to a compliance with the other's wish." Mrs. Chamberlain and an only child, Anna Irwin Chamberlain, survive.

It was in his home that Mr. Chamberlain found his greatest delight. His home-life was to him rest and recreation and benediction. There his gentleness, his unselfishness, his humor, his high spirits, his amiable wisdom, were given free play. To his home his friends were always welcomed. Unconsciously he drew others to him, and instinctively he adapted himself to them. His was an ever-varying, inexhaustible attractiveness.

Nor were his enthusiasms bounded by even his profession and his home. He was a discriminating bibliophile and an accomplished, successful collector. By quiet, assiduous watching and waiting, as well as by courageous competitive purchase, he made himself the possessor of what was said to be the foremost collection of American first editions. He had also a choice general library. To his books he gave an almost paternal care. His hand caressed them. His affection went out to them. He took pains with their appearance. He knew and justly appreciated their contents. When among his books, he could say with Burton in his *Anatomy of Melancholy*, "Here I take my seat, with so lofty a spirit and sweet content, that I pity all our great ones and rich men that know not this happiness."

He was also an experienced, "born" genealogist. He became one of the founders of the Chamberlain Association of America. He was among its wisest councillors and most generous supporters. He believed in an honest pride in ancestry. He put exceeding value on the high incentive which worthy lineage affords. And that, though he well remembered the saying of Plato, "For a person who thinks himself to be somebody, there is nothing more disgraceful than to exhibit himself as held in honor, not on his own account, but for the renown of his forefathers."

Mr. Chamberlain was a faithful citizen. He cared for the best interests of city and state and country. He advocated political integrity of purpose and purity of action. He was not unmindful of the usefulness of political parties, yet he regarded their demands as distinctly subordinate to the claims of the public welfare. His free vote was cast for men of honor. His refined and generous nature, no less than his sound culture and his wide observation, made him the supporter of all that was for the betterment of his fellow men.

Comely, courteous, joyous, with a genius for friendship, he was the light of his beautiful home, a center of attraction among many acquaintances, and an example of perfect uprightness in wide business relations. He was, all in all, a Christian gentleman of rarely noble type.

NECROLOGY

THE Association has lost by death the following members not before reported:

Mrs. Amy Chamberlain Shanks, Round Lake, N. Y., d. January 23, 1905.
Col. Henry Herschel Adams, New York City, d. at Greenwich, Conn., June 25, 1905.
Mr. Eugene G. Chamberlin, Chicago, Ill., d. September 1, 1905.
Mr. John Frederick Chamberlin, Summit, N. J., d. September 14, 1905.
Mr. Edward Watts Chamberlain, Louisville, Ky., d. December 18, 1905.
Mr. James I. Chamberlain, Harrisburg, Pa., d. June 1, 1906.
Miss Henrietta Maria Chamberlaine, Baltimore, Md., d. at Aiken, Cecil Co., Md., December 13, 1906.
Hon. Henry Chamberlain, Three Oaks, Mich., d. February 9, 1907.
Hon. Daniel Henry Chamberlain, West Brookfield, Mass., d. at Charlottesville, Va., April 13, 1907.
Mr. Jacob Aimes Chamberlain, Warwick, N. Y., d. June 28, 1907.

AMY CHAMBERLAIN SHANKS, who died January 23, 1905, in the fifty-fifth year of her age, was a daughter of William Young Chamberlain, a physician of Amenia, N. Y.; a granddaughter of Oliver E. Chamberlain, a colonel in the War of 1812; and a great-granddaughter of Capt. William Chamberlain, an officer in the War of the Revolution. In the twenty-third year of her age—about 1873—she married Charles Gove Shanks. Though of a prominent family in Louisville—owner of slaves, he had enlisted to fight for the Union as a private in the 22d Kentucky Volunteers; and had later served as First Lieutenant of the 7th Kentucky Volunteers, and as aide-de-camp in 1865 on the staff of Brigadier-General M. K. Lawler. Five children were born to them; two died in childhood, three daughters survive. During the twelve years of her widowhood, Mrs. Shanks lived in her country home at Round Lake, Saratoga County, N. Y. She wrote the "Home and Household" columns of the *New York Tribune*, known in the old *Weekly Tribune* under the title, "For the Family Circle," and found in the Sunday edition on the "Home and Society" page. Under the name Helena Rowe—her grandmother's name—she was a salaried contributor to *Good Housekeeping*, when Clark W. Bryan was its editor. In the palmy days of the *New York Ledger*, its publisher, Mr. Bowen, offered her double the salary she was then receiving from the *Tribune*, if she would write exclusively for the *Ledger*, but she refused and retained her connection with the *Tribune* until her death. She wrote magazine articles on other subjects than domestic science. She was especially a nature-lover, and spent many hours studying the wild song-birds near her country home. Her daughter, Maria G. Shanks, continues her work for the *Tribune*.

EUGENE GERLEY CHAMBERLIN was born at Northfield, Mich., November 24, 1848. His parents, Tenbroek and Celinda (Todd) Chamberlin, removed to Monroe, Mich., where he was educated in the public schools. Entering the insurance business early in life, he became identified with the Hartford Steam Boiler Insurance and Inspection Company in 1879, serving in its Boston office until 1893, when he was transferred to its Northwestern department as Assistant Manager of the business in eight states with office and headquarters in Chicago. This position he retained until his death. While a thorough business man, he was also of most gentle disposition and of extreme courtesy, winning and retaining the esteem of all who made his acquaintance. He was a member of the Church of the Messiah in Chicago, and of the Unitarian Club of that city. He was a most devoted husband, and, preferring the quiet of his own home, was not a clubman. He was a Republican, but not a politician. He was interred in Pine Grove Cemetery at Brunswick, Me., the native town of his widow, Emma (Wing) Chamberlin. The earliest paternal ancestor of Eugene Chamberlin in America was, probably, Henry, who came, in 1638, from Hingham, England, and settled at Hingham, New England. The line of ascent is, Eugene,[10] Tenbroek,[9] Tenbroek,[8] Tenbroek,[7] William,[6] Lewis,[5] John[4] (?), Henry,[3] John,[2] Henry.[1] On the maternal side he was descended from Edward Dotey of the *Mayflower*, and Thomas Clark, who came on the *Ann* in 1623.

EDWARD WATTS CHAMBERLAIN, born in Salem, Mass., removed, in 1859, to Louisville, Ky., engaging in the wholesale grocery business; and became later financial manager and confidential clerk of H. D. Newcomb and Company, and of their successor, the Newcomb-Buchanan Company. For the last thirty years of his life, he was the treasurer and selling agent of the Indiana Cotton Mills at Cannelton, Indiana. He was, also, the financial agent, at Louisville, of Victor Newcomb of New York. He married, in 1869, Louise Osborn, daughter of Kendall Osborn, of Peabody, Mass. His wife and one son, William Chamberlain, a member of this Association, survive him. Miss Sarah P. Chamberlain, of Salem, also a member of this Association, is his sister. Long identified with the activities of Louisville, and "maintaining the highest code of commercial ethics," he won the respect of his associates, and many tributes to the integrity of his character. The *Louisville Evening Post* says: "The Cannelton Mills are located at Cannelton, though the business headquarters are in Louisville. On a shipment of cotton from Memphis to Cannelton Mr. Chamberlain discovered it had been billed at an underweight. He investigated the matter, ascertained the amount received, and sent the railroad a check for the difference. 'Something,' said the railroad agent, 'we never had done to us before—nor since.' It is an index to Mr. Chamberlain's character. He was careful of details, and as scrupulously honest in small transactions as in great ones. . . . He has lived many years in Louisville, he has seen its business grow to large proportions, and he has had his share in that growth, illustrating in his own career the fact that a good name is better than riches, and that a successful business is not inconsistent with the strictest probity."

MR. JACOB AIMES CHAMBERLAIN

NECROLOGY

JACOB AIMES CHAMBERLAIN, the youngest son of John C. and Mary Aimes Chamberlain, was born in New York City, September 20, 1846. When a young man he entered business with his father, who died at Warwick in 1891. He built in 1889, a beautiful summer residence at Warwick, Orange County, N. Y., and made it permanently his home when he retired from active business in 1893. The *Warwick Advertiser*, July 4, 1907, said: "Since he became a resident of the village he was interested in its progress and its improvement, and he was well known and sincerely respected by our people. His death, at a comparatively early age, is a distinct loss to Warwick. He was a member of the Colonial Club, the Union League Club, and the Quill Club of New York, but he was essentially a man devoted to his home, his family, and his friends, and entertained frequently at his beautiful home here." In 1871 he married Frances Reading, of New York City. He is survived by his wife and four children,—Amy, wife of Rev. J. Holmes McGuinness of Chester, N. Y.; Harry F. Chamberlain of New York City; Helen, wife of Clifford S. Beattie of Warwick, and Dr. Aimes R. Chamberlain, just completing his service at Mount Sinai Hospital. Mr. Roswell W. Chamberlain, a member of this Association, is his brother. Two sisters, Mrs. Albert S. Roe and Mrs. Francis W. Otherman, live in New York City.

JACOB S. BROWN, the husband of one of our early members, died at his home in La Grange, Ind., October 27, 1906. He was the son of Abijah and Maria (Shoff) Brown, and was born at West Almond, Allegany County, N. Y., March 22, 1829. He married for his second wife, October 17, 1865, Sarah Minerva Chamberlain, daughter of Dr. Joseph W. Chamberlain, of Elkhart, Ind. They lived three years in Gilead, Mich., and afterwards at La Grange, where he purchased his father's interest in a drug store. After the fire of 1877 he supervised building operations, including the manufacture of brick. He constructed, in 1878, in a brick block "the first adequate auditorium, stage and scenery that the town had had for public entertainments." With the help of his brother-in-law, Capt. Orville T. Chamberlain, of Elkhart, he secured for La Grange an east and west railroad. He was interested in the development of large tracts of coal and lumber lands in Dickinson County, Va. The *La Grange Standard*, November 1, 1906, said: "He was a man of remarkable foresight, keen in the perception of opportunity, prompt and vigorous in action. . . . He was a sturdy fighter for whatever he judged his own rights as a citizen and business man. He stood up for his own town and for his own end of the town, and men respected him for it. . . . He was brave, clean and true—ever cheerful and undaunted and ready to help. In politics he was a Republican. He had no membership in any organization but the Masonic order. He was tolerant of religious opinions, and had faith in the realities of eternal life." Two of his children are of Chamberlain descent,—Frederick J. Brown of La Grange, and Caroline Gertrude, wife of Dr. H. B. Roberts, of Highland Park, Ill.

JUDGE A. O. FURST died at his home in Bellefonte, Pa., in November, 1906, after a long, painful illness. His widow, Mrs. Caroline W. Furst, long a member of this Association, is the sister of Mr. James I. Chamberlain, of Harrisburg, Pa., who died in June, 1906. As a barrister Judge Furst chose never to take a case for a client unless he intended to win it. Hence his legal career was an almost unbroken success. He had a large and lucrative practice in Philadelphia, as well as in the various courts of central Pennsylvania. Even New York City interests sought his advice. His judicial decisions, as President Judge of the Centre County Courts, from 1884 to 1894, were almost never reversed. He was a strong support to the religious and charitable interests of Bellefonte.

HON. HENRY CHAMBERLAIN

February 9, 1907, closed the record of four score and three years in the life of the late Hon. Henry Chamberlain, of Three Oaks, Mich. Born at Pembroke, N. H., March 17, 1824, to Moses and Mary (Foster) Chamberlain, he was one of five children, the two other sons being the late Judge Mellen Chamberlain of Chelsea, and the late Hon. William Chamberlain of Michigan. At the age of twelve he entered his father's store in Concord, the capital of the state, and was engaged in merchandising, with the exception of two terms spent at Pembroke Academy, until 1843. Then he removed with his father to Michigan, settling in the township of New Buffalo, which later became, for a period, the terminus of the Michigan Central Railroad, the traffic to Chicago being by lake from this point. The family were pioneers in a wooded wilderness, and the young man, already interested in civic and national affairs, had the strenuous and valuable training which the occupations of woodsman, farmer, merchant, wood contractor, township supervisor, mail agent, land agent, and legislator gave.

Throughout his life his interest in the betterment of government caused him to devote much thought to economic and political questions. "As a young man he espoused the principles of Thomas Jefferson, and for over half a century he preached them and worked for them," attending, according to the *Grand Rapids Press* (1907), "every local convention in his district and practically every state convention of his party during the last fifty years." All who value republican government, and who realize how essential political parties are to its successful working, must feel that Michigan owes him a debt of gratitude for striving to maintain a high standard of intelligence and honor in the minority party of a state so overwhelmingly Republican that he was forced to sacrifice his personal ambition to his political principles. Although a pronounced partisan, his views were so liberal that he was highly esteemed by all thinking men of his acquaintance. Few men have known the moving spirits of the state as did he. Beginning with the first governor, Lewis Cass, he knew all but one of his successors, and most of them intimately. He was a member of the State Legislature (1849); received the vote of the Democratic party six times for Representative or Senator

Hon. Henry Chamberlain

in the United States Congress, and once for governor (1874); and was Grand Master of Michigan Masons in 1872. For over forty years he was a member of the Congregational church at Three Oaks. His interest in scientific farming was always active. In 1848 he was one of the founders of the Michigan State Agricultural Society, and for a number of years was a member of the State Board of Agriculture, and one of the Board of Control of the Michigan Agricultural College, to which he gave much attention. In practical farming he cleared and brought under cultivation more than one thousand acres of land. His great store of knowledge was always available to his friends and neighbors, and left many an impress for high aims and fair dealing in the community which grew up around him.

Mr. Chamberlain was twice married. His first wife, Sarah J. Nash, living little more than a year, passed away in 1851, leaving a son, the first child born in the village of Three Oaks. In 1856 he remarried, and his wife, Rebecca Van Devanter (Ames), lived until 1896. Of this marriage two daughters and one son survive him. All of his children are members of this Association.

His academic training was meagre, but his wonderful memory, coupled with a highly developed analytic habit of mind, made him a cultured and scholarly man. At the age of thirteen he read Blackstone, and throughout life he had at his command the principles of the common law. In the same way history, science, and belle-lettres were absorbed.

Among the many tributes were: "He was a splendid type of public-spirited citizenship;" he was noted for "absolute honesty in all things private and public, and fearlessness in the doing of what he considered right." "His life will ever be held as a sweet memory by the people of this state. Berrien County will keenly feel the loss of the one man entitled to be called 'Berrien's Grand Old Man.'"

JOHN FREDERICK CHAMBERLIN

JOHN FREDERICK CHAMBERLIN, who died at his summer home, Craigville, Mass., was born, October 22, 1843, in Old New York, in what was then known as Chelsea, near the site of the present Grand Opera House. He was a descendant of Thomas Chamberlain of Woburn, Mass., 1644, and inherited Revolutionary blood from both sides of the family. His grandfather, Abel Chamberlin of Plymouth, Mass., who served from 1779 to 1783, was obliged to enlist three times (his first two companies being mustered out) in order to carry out his purpose to fight for his country. Described at the time of his enlistment as eighteen years of age, and five feet two inches in height, literally he grew up in the service, as he returned at the close of the war six feet in stature. He merits the distinction of being one of a very few Revolutionary family heroes, not officers. On his mother's side John Frederick Chamberlin was descended from Maj. Robert Warner of Middletown, Conn., who was commissioned by John Hancock in 1776, and served till the close of the war. Major Warner was a member of the Society of the Cincinnati, and a friend of Washington. Mr. Chamberlin's father, Jacob Chamberlin, came from Concord, N. H., and established an importing business in New York City, in the management of which he crossed the ocean many times—both before and after the use of steam vessels. He was a man of remarkable energy and business ability, and it was owing to his exertions and his personal relations with Daniel Webster, Henry Clay and Theodore Frelinghuysen, that a number of reforms were introduced into the Custom House methods of that time. From his father, Mr. Chamberlin inherited much of his force, foresight, and shrewdness, as well as a manner which was at once polished and attractive. His mother, Mary Elizabeth (Spear), come from Middletown, Conn., and was related to the Harrington and Warner families of that place. She was a remarkably gifted woman, with a wonderful memory for literature, and a fine sense for whatever was best in art, poetry, or music. Above and beyond all this she was a most lovely Christian character.

Mr. Chamberlin's family moved from New York to Jersey City when he was quite young, and he received his education at private schools in that city. Some of his school companions have since become prominent in banking and railroad affairs; one, at the head of three of the largest railroads of the country, is at present one of the most important factors in the financial community.

Mr. Chamberlin entered Wall Street as a clerk in the house of Winslow, Lanier and Company in 1861, working his way up through the various grades until 1887, when he became a partner of the house—continuing his connection as a member of the firm till his death. During this forty-four years' experience in the Street he had to face many and difficult financial problems, passing through some of the greatest upheavals the country has ever known—the great panics of 1869,

1873, 1884, 1890, 1893, and 1901. He was a   1 Room in the panic of 1869 (Black Friday), and by his firmness and skill brought out his contracts without loss. From 1883 to 1884 his firm sold 50,000,000 of West Shore bonds, and had to face the panic of that year, which included the failure of Grant and Ward, the closing of the Marine Bank, and the receivership of the West Shore Railroad. During all these troublous times his faith and courage never faltered. He believed always that firmness, skill, and patience bring success out of conditions that menace disaster.

He was a member of the New York Stock Exchange, Vice President and Director of the N. K. Fairbanks Company of Chicago, Trustee of the Washington Trust Company of New York, and Director and Chairman of the Executive Committee of the American Cotton Oil Company. In this position, which he held for eleven years, as the practical head of a reorganizing bureau, he accomplished some of his most difficult and successful work. To bring the affairs of a large corporation with diversified interests, extended over a large part of the United States, into harmonious relations, so that disorganized parts become a complete and organized whole, so that diffusion and loss change to concentration and profit, is a task that calls forth the best and highest qualities of a leader of men. The appreciation of his fellow directors appears in the following resolution taken from the minutes of the company, October 3, 1905.

"Resolved—That the Board of Directors of The American Cotton Oil Company have learned with deep sorrow of the death of J. Frederick Chamberlin, who has been a member of this Board and of its Executive Committee since 1894.

"Mr. Chamberlin was a man of ripe judgment, whose active co-operation in the management was of great value to this Organization. He was a thorough and persistent worker, giving much attention to detail and possessing a liberal and comprehensive mind. His courtesy to others, and the careful consideration given to their views, made his intercourse with his fellow members as agreeable as his large experience in affairs and firmness of will rendered him pre-eminently useful. He was of a genial and happy disposition, which endeared him to all his associates."

At Summit, N. J., where he made his home, he was Vice President and Director of the Summit Building and Loan Association, a Director of the Summit National Bank, and a Trustee of the Fresh Air Home. Always interested in the public schools, he served for six years as President of the School Board—retiring only on account of ill health. His long business experience and financial sagacity were always at the command of his fellow townsmen for any useful work, and were always sought for and fully appreciated by his associates. He was a member of Calvary Episcopal Church, giving his voice and attention for many years to its choir service. The vestry at their meeting, September 17th, speak as follows:

"The Vestry of Calvary Church desire to place on record their high esteem for their late associate, Mr. J. Frederick Chamberlin, and their keen sense of his loss to the Church and the community.

"For twen[...] [Cha]mberlin had been a faithful member of this parish, always taking [...] [wo]rk and welfare. For ten years he was a member of this Vestry, and [...] one of its wardens.

"In token of their respect the Vestry desire to attend the funeral services in a body, and they extend to Mrs. Chamberlin and her family their warm sympathy in this great bereavement."

From a letter written by the manager of the N. K. Fairbanks Company, a younger associate in the work, is taken the following extract, showing the kindly side of Mr. Chamberlin's character. He says: "I have good reason to know something of his character, and I shall always cherish the recollection of his kindness and patience accorded me on many occasions, neither shall I ever forget the wise and gentle counsel that he always extended to me. His loss is indeed a personal one for me as well as for the company." A man who makes such a record as John Frederick Chamberlin for character and ability, leaves a reputation worthy of the ancestors from whom he descended, and of this Association to which he considered it an honor to belong. While recognizing the full value of the brilliant qualities which guaranteed him success in business and civic life, it is pleasant to remember that in his character they were always mingled with the lovable attributes of kindness, courtesy, and care for others. These, when much of life's work is forgotten, will ever rise in fragrant memory, and like a wreath never fading may fitly crown his epitaph.

Mr. Chamberlin is survived by a widow and three daughters, Mrs. May Chamberlin Berry, Mrs. Jessie Chamberlin Moore, and Miss Edna Winslow Chamberlin; also by two brothers, Emerson and George W. Chamberlin, all members of this Association.

SUMMIT, N. J., August, 1906.

Hon. Daniel Henry Chamberlain
Governor of South Carolina, 1874-1877

HON. DANIEL H. CHAMBERLAIN

DANIEL HENRY CHAMBERLAIN was born on a farm in West Brookfield, Worcester County, Mass., June 23, 1835, the ninth of ten children, and shared the home life which his brother, Rev. Leander Trowbridge Chamberlain, D. D., describes so pleasingly in the Annual Report of this Association for 1904-5 (p. 36). He studied for a few months at the Academy in Amherst, Mass., beginning the study of Latin and Greek in 1849 and 1850; and part of a year at Phillips Academy, Andover, in 1854; and completed his preparation for college at the High School in Worcester under Homer B. Sprague and Wolcott Calkins in 1856 and 1857. With his friend Walter Allen, later of the *Boston Daily Advertiser* and of the *Boston Herald*, and the historian of Governor Chamberlain's administration in South Carolina, he founded at the High School a literary society, "The Eucleia," which still remains. He taught school each winter from 1852 to 1856, and at the High School in Worcester for a year after his graduation. He entered Yale College in 1858, and four years later, in 1862, received the A. B. degree, holding the fourth place in general scholarship in a class of one hundred and ten members, and winning the De Forest medal, the great prize of the course for English composition and oratory. He was elected the orator of his class. A Yale professor of that period declared that Chamberlain and John C. Calhoun had the most brilliant minds of all who had come under his notice. A classmate has said of him, "He was easily the most influential leader of his class." He entered the Harvard Law School, where Secretary Fairchild, a fellow student, remembers him as the "ablest man in that school of his time." How he left his studies to enlist as Second Lieutenant of the Fifth Massachusetts Cavalry, a regiment of colored men, is told in the Annual Report of this Association for 1903 (p. 66). His interest in "the struggle for the Union and for Freedom," as he called it, was always deep. In the Presidential election of 1860 he voted for Abraham Lincoln, and whenever possible he listened to the great speakers on abolition,—he himself has said he must have heard Wendell Phillips speak in public more than fifty times. As to his army career, nothing has been learned which does not appear in the Annual Report for 1903. He held the rank of Captain when he was mustered out of the service in December, 1865.

Early in January, 1866, he went to Charleston, S. C., to settle the affairs of a classmate, James Pierpont Blake, of New Haven, drowned at Edisto Island. While so engaged, he visited the Sea Islands near Charleston, where he was led to engage in cotton planting. In the autumn of 1867 he was chosen a member of the Constitutional Convention called under the reconstruction acts, and took his seat in that body in January, 1868. He was a member of its Judiciary Committee, and was influential in all its deliberations. He so acquitted himself that all the friends of the new Constitution desired him to be one of the state officers to establish in practical operation the new organization of government. The office of Attorney-General, being in the line of his chosen profession, was the only one he would consent to take; and to this he was chosen, and held it for four years continuously, 1868 to 1872. This Attorney-General, whose law studies had been prematurely broken off, who had never had a day's practice in the courts, almost immediately found himself pitted against some of the foremost lawyers of a community, always distinguished for the learning and ability of its Bar, in the trial of causes of great moment, involving the highest constitutional and legal questions, a strenuous endeavor being made to secure fulfillment of the prediction that the new State could not live. It was soon discovered by them that their inexperienced opponent was a man in whom it was not wise to presume any weakness that could be overcome by tireless industry and sound thinking. When Chamberlain was elected Attorney-General, Franklin J. Moses, Jr., was elected Governor. "It is a curious fact that Moses, member of an old South Carolina family, carefully brought up in the traditions of the class to which he was born, should actually have been involved in scandalous corruption of the ignorant negro legislators, and have gone out of office quite disgraced," while the memorialist of Governor Chamberlain is able to write, "It is certain that amidst the unfortunate and disgraceful events of that unhappy time, which were afterward so thoroughly opened to the light of day, no taint of dishonor or suspicion of peculation, or of what we have come to know as 'graft,' ever attached to him." With his "predilections in favor of the negro race," gained as an officer of a negro regiment in war times, he became by a moral necessity a leader in the effort to secure to them, "their advantage under the new amendments to the constitution." As Judge P. Emory Aldrich said, "In these trying [reconstruction] times Chamberlain's conduct has been as heroic as anything we have had in the war."

He was Governor of the state of South Carolina from January, 1874, to April, 1877, when the withdrawal of federal troops after a contested election forced him to leave the office. He never forgot nor forgave the withdrawal of support from him by the national government in March, 1877, and truthfully maintained that if he was not elected Governor of South Carolina in 1876, then the Hayes presidential electors were not chosen, and President Hayes clouded his own title to the presidency by withdrawing his support. As Charles Francis Adams has pointed out, the leader of the forces of the state opposed to him was "disposed to stop at absolutely no action necessary to secure the white man's ascendency. . . . It was a very grim situation. . . . Further to have contended would have been to challenge destruction." The same writer points out that the governments organized according to the Congressional plan of reconstruction had already disappeared from every state except South Carolina, and that this system continued there "by virtue solely of Governor D. H. Chamberlain's vigor, and the reformatory life his personality had infused into the moribund body," and that he, "struggling desperately to accomplish the impossible, was the one redeeming factor in the South Carolina situation." Yet though he lost the office, his efforts bore fruit.

Mr. James Ford Rhodes writes: "During his canvass in 1874 he had said: 'The work of reform will be a constant struggle. . . . If in my two years as Governor I can even "turn the tide," I shall be more than rewarded.' This indeed he accomplished. He began the redemption of South Carolina; it was completed under Democratic auspices." (History of the United States, VII, 167.) Later Mr. Chamberlain came to believe that the end he desired was attained more fully under Governor Wade Hampton, a native South Carolinian, and the newly organized Democratic party, than it could have been under his own hampered leadership, and his memories of South Carolina and its leading men were not embittered by his personal disappointment.

To attempt even a brief outline of his career as Attorney-General and Governor of South Carolina is not feasible within the limits of this brief sketch, yet the compiler cannot resist the desire to include a few quotations. Mr. Chamberlain said: "My highest ambition as Governor has been to make the ascendancy of the Republican party in South Carolina compatible with the attainment and maintenance of as high and pure a tone in the administration of public affairs as can be exhibited in the proudest Democratic State of the South." In his "Reconstruction, Political and Economic," William A. Dunning has recently written: "In 1874 Daniel H. Chamberlain, a Massachusetts man of great eloquence and ability, had been elected governor to succeed the unspeakable Moses. By bold and spectacular proceedings he effected very considerable reforms in the State administration, incurring thereby the vindictive animosity of the shameless crew in his own party whose vicious practices were interfered with. . . . Chamberlain was the only carpet-bagger governor in the South who had shown both the will and the ability to secure any measure of purity in State administration." That his efforts were recognized at the time is shown by the Democratic *News and Courier* of Charleston. In January, 1875, it said he sent to his Legislature a special message full of "wise, prudent, and just" recommendations; also, in May of the same year, that he "is as true as steel, in the fight against public dishonesty. . . . It is due to Mr. Chamberlain that, for the first time in six years, there was no considerable stealing during the legislative session, and that not one swindling bill became a law." It spoke of "his scholarly messages, his patriotic utterances, his unfailing tact and courtesy." It also said: "In the light of his acts, since he has been Governor, we say now that, however much appearances were against him, it is morally impossible that he should have been either facile or corrupt. . . . Governor Chamberlain, therefore, richly deserves the confidence of the people of this State. The people of South Carolina, who have all at stake, who see and hear what persons outside the State cannot know, are satisfied of Governor Chamberlain's honesty. . . . By and with the aid of the Conservatives, Governor Chamberlain and the small band of honest Republicans defeated the thieves in every engagement. But the men whom he has thrown down, and who did not want or expect reform, are wild with rage and despair." A paper by one of his political opponents in South Carolina, written recently at the request of Charles

Francis Adams, has been published in the "Proceedings of the Massachusetts Historical Society" for May, 1907. Though tinged slightly by the Southern gentleman's well known difficulty in recognizing integrity of thought and according the highest moral rank to those differing from him in opinion so long as they continue to differ, it is nevertheless a noteworthy tribute to Governor Chamberlain's integrity of purpose, and in connection with the newspaper extract just given, an interesting evidence of how nearly Governor Chamberlain succeeded in uniting in the support of his administration the best men of both parties. "He was elected Governor in 1874: his administration was marked by great improvement over those which had preceded him, but he was hampered by the Legislature, and by many who had been, and still were, his political associates. This was specially marked in the election of two of the most objectionable characters in the State as Judges. The Governor denounced the action of the General Assembly, and refused to issue commissions, thus keeping these men out of office. . . . He rendered other great services, among which was the adjustment of the State bond debt, which he effected through a settlement with the bondholders. Late in '75, or early in '76, he appointed a Board to scrutinize and pass on money claims against the State, of which there were many, fraudulent and otherwise, outstanding. . . . In 1876 Governor Chamberlain was a candidate for re-election; and, accepting as a reformer, had at first the support of most of the press and of nearly all the recognized leaders of the Democrats, or white people, of the State. . . . Almost every man in the State prominent in political affairs had been already committed to the Chamberlain policy. The National Democratic Executive Committee had adopted the same lines, and their agents were here at work; but General Wade Hampton before going to his plantation in Mississippi, had assured some of us that if the 'straight-out' 'home-rule' policy were adopted he would go into line, and fight with all the power that was in him. . . . On 28th June, 1876, the centennial of the Battle of Fort Moultrie was celebrated. Governor Chamberlain was the orator, and many thought his speech on that occasion had made his nomination certain. . . . The 'straight-outs' carried the convention in August by a small majority,—three, I think. The vote was then made unanimous. . . . The action of our convention was a bitter disappointment to Governor Chamberlain. . . . We won on election day, carrying the State ticket by a small majority,—only a few hundreds. . . . In December the General Assembly convened. Hampton and Chamberlain each took the oath of office and declared himself Governor. . . . Born when the passions of prejudice were in their rapid growth, he was nurtured with them, as moral food, and entered the army when the bloody Civil War was raging. It would have been more than human to cast off the past in a moment, and to be a reformer in the party and against the principles which he had imbibed as gospel, before they had been tested by the lessons of experience;—but he was endowed with high traits; he was a patriot, he was a searcher after truth, and, when he believed it found, he was brave enough to declare it, without regard to danger or its inconsistency with his past. He loved his country, and was to the end loyal to the State of his adoption, and came to love the men who had crushed his highest hope in the zenith of his public life. He was a student, a worker, and a thinker; and when he discovered that he had dreamed of the impossible, he frankly said so, and defended the men who had opposed him. He was pure of heart and of a pure mind; and in time he rose above the clouds. I remember him with love and respect."

After Governor Chamberlain's public life in South Carolina had come to its close, he entered a prominent law firm in New York City. He was engaged in conspicuous cases in the state courts and before the Supreme Court; but he had permanently sapped his physical health in anxious public life, and illness, with temporary disability, came upon him. Obliged to give up, he travelled in Europe. Afterward he accepted less exacting terms of professional work as Receiver of the South Carolina Railroad in behalf of the bondholders, and in that capacity he made his home temporarily in Charleston until he was peremptorily ordered by his physician to lead an easier existence.

Returning to West Brookfield, he settled upon the site of his birthplace, where he interested himself in his farming operations as well as in local affairs and history. He became one of the best informed antiquarians of his neighborhood, and President of the Quaboag Historical Society. From February, 1900, until his death he was a member of the Massachusetts Historical Society, and contributed several papers to its Proceedings. Although forced to curtail his energies in the more strenuous channels of life, he always maintained his interest in public affairs; and a constant comment thereon in the public prints showed to the last his great power of clear and trenchant criticism. He became a publicist. He was an ardent civil-service reformer and anti-imperialist. Articles written by him appeared in the files of the *North American Review*, the *Atlantic Monthly*, the *Harvard Law Review*, the *Yale Law Journal*, the *American Law Review*, the *American Historical Review*, and elsewhere. The University of South Carolina gave him the degree of LL. D. in 1873; and upon the founding of the Law School of Cornell University, he was appointed non-resident professor of Constitutional Law.

In 1869 he married Alice Cornelia Ingersoll, daughter of George W. Ingersoll of Bangor, Me. She died during the time of his New York practice. Two of his six sons survive him,—Julian Ingersoll Chamberlain of Boston, and Paul C. Chamberlain of Washington, D. C. Forced to seek a milder climate than New England, he was separated from his nearest of kin during his last days, but was among friends of his own name to whom he had greatly endeared himself. Neither affliction nor pain could conquer his mental energy and power. When so weak that he "could only write a dozen or twenty words, and then give up exhausted and panting," he labored "during five long days" on an article, which when finished showed no trace of weakness or fragmentariness. He died at Charlottesville, Va., April 13, 1907, and was interred at West Brookfield, Mass.

He was one of the early members of this Association, and contributed one hundred dollars toward the establishment of our Bureau of Genealogy. It was a matter of regret that he was able to be present at only one of our annual gatherings. Much of the material for this sketch has been taken, frequently verbatim, from the memorial by Edward H. Gilbert in the "Proceedings of the Massachusetts Historical Society" for October, 1907. The most lengthy sketch of his life is contained in a book entitled "Governor Chamberlain's Administration in South Carolina" (544 pages), written by Walter Allen, a life-long friend.

PERSONAL RECORDS

HON. ABIRAM CHAMBERLAIN

Hon. Abiram Chamberlain, former Governor of Connecticut, and a prominent banker in New England, the guest of this Association at its annual reunion in 1907, was born in the town of Colebrook, Litchfield County, Connecticut, December 7, 1837. His ancestors on both sides were of the oldest and purest New England stock, one of the most distant on his father's side being Jacob Chamberlain, who was born in Massachusets in 1673. On his mother's side Mr. Chamberlain is descended from Henry and Eulalia Burt. Mr. Chamberlain's father was Deacon Abiram Chamberlain, a most skillful and experienced civil engineer and surveyor, a man of great uprightness and stability of character, and widely known for his attractive personality. Mr. Chamberlain's mother was Sophronia Burt.

After receiving a public school education, Mr. Chamberlain studied at Williston Seminary, Easthampton, Mass., where he made a special study of civil engineering, his father's calling. In 1856 the family moved to New Britain, where Mr. Chamberlain learned the trade of rule making, and practiced civil engineering with his father. He soon abandoned this course to become a teller in the New Britain National Bank. This step was the turning point of his career, for Mr. Chamberlain was destined to be identified with finance instead of engineering. In 1867 he moved to Meriden, and became cashier of the Home National Bank. In 1881 he became president of that bank, a position which he still holds.

Though few men have had more thorough experience in banking than Mr. Chamberlain, he has found time for many other interests, as his many public offices have shown. He was at one time city auditor and a member of the City Government, and has represented his town in the State Legislature. In 1901 and 1902 he was state comptroller, and in September, 1902, he was nominated for governor of the state of Connecticut, and elected by a large majority. From the time his first address won public applause, he was in high favor, not only because of his dignity and executive ability, but for his kindness and geniality. Soon after his election the Waterbury Trolley Strike occurred, and the decision and mastery with which Governor Chamberlain quelled the disturbance proved him thoroughly worthy of his great trust.

Mr. Chamberlain has always been a promoter of everything possible for the welfare of Meriden, and he is actively interested in many of its leading institutions. He is vice-president of the Meriden Savings Bank, director in the Meriden Hospital, in the Meriden Cutlery Company, in the Edward Miller and Company; also a director of the Stanley Works in New Britain. He is a member of the Home and Colonial Clubs of Meriden, the Hartford Club, the Union League Club of

New Haven, and the Metabetchouan Fishing and Game Club of Canada. He has served five years in the State Militia, and is fond of outdoor life, especially golf, baseball, and fishing. In politics he is a Republican, and in religious affiliation a Congregationalist.

In 1872 Mr. Chamberlain was married to Charlotte E. Roberts. Two sons have been born to them, both of whom are now living, Albert Roberts and Harold Burt.

Mr. Chamberlain may be called a self-made man in the best sense of the word—in everything that he has undertaken, he has succeeded; although he has never sought political office, he has been honored with the governorship of the state. In the business of banking he has attained to a position of importance, and has been complimented by being elected president of the Connecticut Bankers' Association, and a vice-president, representing the state of Connecticut, in the American Bankers' Association. Perhaps the best tribute to his mental capability was the honorary degree of LL. D., conferred upon him by Wesleyan University, in 1903.

THOMAS CHAMBERLAIN

THOMAS CHAMBERLAIN, one of the charter members of the Chamberlain Association and Treasurer of the society since its organization, was born at Worcester, Mass., June 4, 1835, the next youngest of eleven children of General Thomas Chamberlain of that city, and sixth in descent from the emigrant William Chamberlain of Woburn, Mass., through three successive Jacobs born at Billerica, Medford and Newton, respectively, and John of Worcester, the father of General Thomas. His mother, Hannah Blair, daughter of Robert and Elizabeth Blair of Rutland and Worcester, Mass., and second wife of General Thomas Chamberlain, was born at Rutland in 1793, and died at Charlestown, Mass., in 1874. His father, a staunch representative of that dignified type of manhood which flourished in the early half of the last century, was born at Worcester, March 6, 1783, and died at the Chamberlain homestead on Salisbury Street, that city, September 5, 1855, after a life filled with activity and public service, in which he held various positions of trust and responsibility. He was President of the first Common Council of Worcester, Crier of the Court for many years, a trustee of the Worcester Horticultural Society, and a representative to the General Court from 1834 to 1836. He filled most of the military offices of the state from Corporal to Major-General, and from the last office received the title by which he was best known.

Deacon John Chamberlain, father of General Thomas, and grandfather of the subject of this sketch, was born at Worcester, July 22, 1745, took an active and prominent part in the affairs of the town, and died at the Chamberlain homestead, May 31, 1813. He was a deacon of the Worcester Old South Church from 1790 until his death, the term of office of his father and himself covering a period of sixty-one years. By his wife Mary, daughter of Capt. John Curtis of Worcester.

Mr. Thomas Chamberlain

an officer in the French and Indian War, he had four sons and two daughters, and in this branch of the family appeared an unmistakable strain of legal blood, for of the four sons of Deacon Chamberlain there was not one whose calling was not linked to either the practice of the law or its administration in the courts of justice. The eldest, John Curtis, was a successful lawyer in Alstead and Charlestown, N. H., and representative to Congress from New Hampshire. The next younger, Henry Vassal, was likewise a lawyer in New Hampshire (practicing also in Maine), and was later a sheriff and judge in Mobile, Ala. The third, General Thomas, was, as already stated, Crier of the Court, and the fourth, Levi, was Clerk of the Court and County Attorney for Cheshire County, N. H., also state senator. It is not surprising, then, that we should find expressed in the next generation, and that immediately following, a capacity of achievement and strength of personality of more than ordinary degree, manifested in the daughters as well as the sons, and that Robert Horace, youngest son of General Thomas, should be found High Sheriff of Worcester County and Master of the House of Correction, while Harry Richardson, grandson of General Thomas, and son of the Thomas of whom we write, should attain to a place of prominence in the foremost ranks of journalism both in this country and abroad.

The early life of Thomas Chamberlain was spent in Worcester, Mass., where he attended the public and high schools, later attending the Westfield Academy at Westfield, Mass., from which he graduated in 1851. In the latter part of the same year he entered the office of the *Boston Journal*, remaining with that paper but two years, when he took a position with the Bunker Hill Bank of Charlestown, Mass., serving as clerk for three years.

In 1856 he left Charlestown for Peoria, Ill., where he engaged in the general hardware business, conducting also an agency for several insurance companies. It was while here that he made a trip east to participate in that most important of all events, and wedded at Boston, August 31, 1858, Helen Augusta, daughter of Solomon and Joanna Augusta (Flint) Hovey, of Charlestown. Mr. Hovey was at that time president of the largest fire insurance company in Boston, the Mechanics Mutual, and occupied a position of much prominence in the business and commercial life of the city. Returning to Peoria immediately after his marriage, Mr. Chamberlain conducted his business at that point until April 12, 1861, on which day he took final departure for the east to accept a position with what was then the State Bank of Boston, now the State National Bank, for many years located on State Street. Entering as discount clerk, he soon became paying teller, which position he held for a great many years, only a comparatively short time ago, owing to failing health, taking the position of assistant teller, in which capacity he now serves, having completed his forty-sixth year with that institution.

At the age of sixteen Mr. Chamberlain became actively identified with the Congregational Church, and since that time has been a constant member of that denomination. His connection with the Eliot Church of Roxbury, Mass., during his residence in that district from 1863 to 1873, was one of particular activity. Of the church at Hyde Park, Mass., where he has resided since 1873, he is and has been a most enthusiastic and efficient member.

While residing in Peoria a peculiar opportunity presented itself to Mr. Chamberlain to be of assistance to the operatives of a mine not far from the town, who were extremely poor. Being always interested in children, he organized at the mine a Sunday-school, which he personally superintended, there being neither church nor day school in the vicinity at that time. The school was not only attended most eagerly, growing to successful proportions during his stay in the West, but proved the nucleus of what afterward became, and is at the present time, a flourishing church of the Methodist denomination.

While Mr. Chamberlain has always been deeply interested in all worthy institutions, he has never allied himself to any organization outside the church or family association, nor aspired in any way to political or ecclesiastical office. To him the home has been pre-eminent, and his, surely, has been an ideal one. Of his children, three of whom are now living, the eldest, Harry Richardson, is at the present time London Correspondent of the *New York Sun*, having filled successively the positions of Managing Editor of the *New York Press* and of the *Boston Journal* during the years 1888 to 1892; Helen Clare resides at Hyde Park, Mass., and Alice Louise, wife of Nestor W. Davis, resides at Winchester, Mass. Mr. Chamberlain's second child, Alfred Thomas, died at Roxbury, Mass., November 26, 1868, at the age of six years. If there is one thing in particular for which Mr. Chamberlain is noted, it is his uniformly genial and kindly disposition, which is well known to all who enjoy his acquaintance. His sympathies are deep and genuine, and as might well be expected, his friends are many and strong.

Hingham Church.

THE ENGLISH HOME AND ENVIRONMENT OF HENRY CHAMBERLIN OF HINGHAM, MASSACHUSETTS

THROUGH the generosity of Rev. Leander Trowbridge Chamberlain, D. D., of New York, English researches for the Chamberlain family history were commenced August 31, 1899. The direction of the work was entrusted to George W. Chamberlain of Weymouth, Mass. Dr. Chamberlain made only one provision, viz., that the researches be so directed as to secure, if possible, the English history of the family from whom William Chamberlain, the New England immigrant to Billerica, Mass., was descended. For this reason more than three years elapsed before any attempt was made to identify the English home of Henry Chamberlin, the earliest English immigrant of the surname Chamberlain to seek a home in New England.

It was well understood that Henry Chamberlin and his family arrived at Charlestown, Mass., August 10, 1638, and that he came in the ship *Diligent* which sailed from Ipswich, touched at London, and made the port of Charlestown in New England on the last-mentioned date. In the *Diligent* were not fewer than one hundred and thirty-three passengers, who had placed themselves under the leadership of Rev. Robert Peck, rector of the parish of Hingham, County of Norfolk, England, from 1605 to 1637. Among the passengers of the *Diligent* came Daniel Cushing, then about eighteen years of age, subsequently town clerk of Hingham, Mass., serving the town from 1669 to 1700. Late in life, probably after 1680, he wrote in his Diary a "list of such persons as came out of the town of Hingham and towns adjacent, in the County of Norfolk, in the Kingdom of England and settled in New Hingham." Among the items, in a distinct hand, may be read after more than two centuries:

"1638: Henry Chamberlin, shoemaker, his wife and his mother and two children came from Old Hingham and settled at New Hingham—5."

This item, written by Mr. Cushing more than forty years after the event to which he referred and after every person mentioned had passed away except Henry Chamberlin's widow who may have been living in the adjoining town of Hull, may not be absolutely correct so far as numbers go. One of two things is certain, viz., if all of the members of Henry Chamberlin's family came in the *Diligent* with him, there were more than two children, and Mr. Cushing's memory after the lapse of forty years or more was not accurate; if some members of Henry Chamberlin's family came at some other time, the item may be strictly correct. There is good authority for believing that Henry Chamberlin had not fewer than six children who must have been born before he came to Massachusetts.

Turning our attention from New England to the history of the County of Norfolk, we get glimpses of the causes of the immigration of the company. We learn that Rev. Robert Peck, a native of Beccles in the County of Suffolk, graduated at Magdalene College in 1599, took the degree A. M. in 1603, and was ordained presbyter by John, Bishop of Norwich, February 4, 1604. He was inducted over the church at Hingham, January 7, 1605-6. Here he remained for more than thirty years.

On one occasion, we are told, that he catechised his family and sung a psalm in his own house on a Lord's Day evening when some of the neighbors were present, for which Bishop Harsnet enjoined him and all present to do penance, and required each to say, "I confess my errors." Those who refused were excommunicated and required to pay heavy costs. For this and other acts the citizens of Norwich, we are told, presented a complaint against Bishop Harsnet in the House of Commons. The Bishop replied that Mr. Peck had been sent to him by the justices of the peace for holding a conventicle at night; that he had been convicted of nonconformity and of holding conventicles in 1615 and 1617, and that in 1622 he was taken in his own house with twenty-two of his neighbors at a conventicle.

Bishop Harsnet was succeeded by Dr. Matthew Wren, who was Bishop of Norwich from 1635 to 1638. He it was who proposed one hundred and thirty-nine articles, in which are found eight hundred and ninety-seven questions,—"articles to be inquired of within the Diocess of Norwich in the first visitation of Matthew, Lord-bishop of Norwich." These questions were read to the clergy of his Diocese, including the parish of Hingham, and their answers returned to him. On account of his severity with the Puritan clergy of his Diocese, the inhabitants of Ipswich drew up a petition against him, and presented it to the House of Parliament December 22, 1640. He was impeached, and on July 5, 1641, the Committee reported, "That the said Matthew Wren [now] Bishop of Ely hath excommunicated, deprived, or banished, within the space of two years, fifty godly, learned and painful ministers." Among these was Rev. Robert Peck of Hingham. However, we must bear in mind that Bishop Wren was imprisoned in the Tower from this time to 1659.

Turning now to the question from the view-point of the Church of England, we are told that Robert Peck was a "man of a very violent schismatical spirit, that he pulled down the rails and leveled the alter and the whole chancel a foot below the church as it remains to this day [1715], but being prosecuted for it by Bishop Wren he fled the kingdom and went over into New England *with many of his parishioners,* who sold their estates for half their value, and conveyed all their effects to that new plantation, erected a town and colonie by the name of Hingham, where many of their posterity are still [1715] remaining." Continuing, we read that "he promosed never to desert them, but hearing that Bishops were deposed, he left them all to shift for themselves and came to Hingham in the year 1646 after ten years of voluntary banishment. He resumed his rectory and died in 1656." This record was written on the parish register of Hingham, England, by the rector in 1715.

In this environment in an age of intolerance Henry Chamberlin and his family lived until the year 1638. The church of St. Andrew, rebuilt in 1316, which was the center of this conflict, is still standing, a handsome specimen of mediæval architecture.

Having gathered the foregoing facts, the next step was to learn about the actual condition of the Hingham parish registers—the one source of English family history at close range. Turning to that monumental work entitled, "Abstracts from the English Parish Registers," published by the British Government, it was found that the registers of Hingham were reported to begin in 1683—more than half a century after the period of Henry Chamberlin's assumed activity in that parish, and nearly ten years after his death in New England. Knowing that this parish was adjoining to the parish of Attleborough and that the latter was a very old parish, the assumption was made that the former parish was set off from Attleborough after the emigration. An expert record searcher was dispatched to the parish of Attleborough with directions to glean all Chamberlain baptisms, marriages and burials from 1552 to 1700. That report cost a little more than twenty-five dollars and was most disappointing.

Not discouraged, the director of the researches applied himself to a most careful, critical examination of Blomefield's "History of the County of Norfolk" (Vol. 2, p. 424). By the context he became convinced that the author of the article relating to Hingham, must in 1805 or thereabouts have seen the Hingham registers, and that they contained baptisms, marriages, and burials of a much earlier date than 1683. Having concluded that the Hingham registers were much older than represented, a letter was dispatched to Mr. George F. Chamberlain of New York (a descendant of Henry Chamberlin) telling him that in all probability the English home of his ancestor had been discovered, and that with twenty-five dollars much valuable ancestral data could be obtained. Promptly the funds were forwarded and again the expert record searcher was sent into the County of Norfolk to the parish of Hingham.

This report, full of most valuable Chamberlain data, revealed the fact that the Hingham parish registers began in 1600. The results of the search in the registers from 1600 to 1700 are as follows:

1600-01: Johan Chamberlyn daughter of Richard Baptised 25 Jan.
1603: Marie Chamberlyn daughter of Richard baptised 27 Nov.
1604: Johan Chamberlyn buried 5 May.
1606: Dorothy Chamberlyn daughter of Richard baptised 9 June.
1611: Susan Chamberlyn daughter of Robert baptised 2 June.
1613: John Chamberline and Elizabeth Ransome married 24 May.
1616-7: Katterine Chamberline daughter of John baptised (?12) Jan.
1619: Anne daughter of John Chamberline baptised 4 April.
1621: Frances daughter of John Chamberline baptised 17 June.
1621: Richard Chamberline and Merget Polye married 26 August.
1622: George Cooper, taylor, and Susan Chamberline married 23 April.
1623: Richard sone of John Chamberline baptised [date faded] May.
1625: Ellen daughter of John Chamberline baptised 29 May.

1627–8: Thomas base son of Joan Chamberline baptised 17 Feb.
1627–8: Richard son of John Chamberline baptised 16 March.
1629–30: Francis son of John Chamberline baptised 10 Jan.
1629: Susan daughter of Robert Chamberline buried 24 Dec.
1631: Richard son of Richard Chamberline baptised 6 June.
1632: Elizabeth daughter of John Chamberline baptised 5 May.

1632: *Daniel* and *Mary* children of *Henry Chamberline* baptised 15 May.
1632: *Daniel* son of *Henry Chamberline* buried 19 May.
1632: *Mary* daughter of *Henry Chamberline* buried 25 May.
1633: JOHN son of HENRY CHAMBERLINE baptised 15 Nov.

1634: John son of John Chamberline baptised 29 June.
1635–6: Robert and Henry sons of Henry and Grace Chamberline baptised 15 March.
1635: Frances daughter of Edward Chamberline buried 6 Nov.
1635–6: Robert Chamberline buried 11 Jan.
1638: Richard Chamberline, the elder, buried 10 August.
1642: All entries wanting for this year.
1649: Grace Chamberline, widow, buried 3 March.
1656: May 5: John Swatman, widower, and Ann Chamberline, singalwooman, of this town bothe were married acordinge to ye tennor of an Act of Parlyment in that caus made and provyded by brampton Gadinge [Brampton Gordon] Esquire, one of ye Justices of ye Peace for this County in the day and yeare before menshened.
1651–1660: Baptisms and burials wanting.
1664–1683: All baptisms, marriages and burials wanting.
1698: Mary Chamberlain, widow, buried 17 June.

These abstracts confirm the fact that Henry Chamberlin lived in the parish of Hingham before coming to New England. It is a matter of regret that the parish registers do not show the baptisms of his elder children, nor his marriage, nor his baptism and with that his father's name. It seems probable that before 1632 he lived in some other parish, where may be found these data. Among the parishes most likely to have the other data, suggestion may be made of Wymondham and Barnham-Broom.

Our English pedigree shows that Edward Chamberleyn, Lord of the Manor of Barnham Broome in 1567, had a brother Henry. This is the earliest mention of the name Henry in the County of Norfolk that has been found. After 1650 the name Henry occurs in several parishes of this county. The diary of Rev. Peter Hobart of Hingham, Mass., shows that the name of Henry Chamberlin's widowed mother was Christian, and that she died at Hingham, Mass., April 19, 1659, aged eighty-one years. Hence she was born about 1578.

March, 1907.

GEORGE W. CHAMBERLAIN.
LEANDER T. CHAMBERLAIN.

HENRY CHAMBERLIN AND HIS DESCENDANTS

By George Walter Chamberlain, M. S.,

Member New England Historic Genealogical Society

My studies on the descendants of Henry Chamberlin of Hull, Mass., from 1662 to 1674, were begun in 1891 and have been continued to the present time. Through the courtesy of the late Hon. Mellen Chamberlain, LL. D., I was able to commence with an exact copy of his Chamberlain data, which he had gathered between 1865 and 1891. Upon removing to the vicinity of Boston in 1895, I pursued my investigations in the library of the New England Historic Genealogical Society which contains the most complete collection of American genealogy in existence. To the librarians of this Society, the late Mr. John Ward Dean and his successor Mr. William Prescott Greenlaw, I am indebted for assistance, advice, and encouragement. In 1899—two years after the Chamberlain Association of America was organized—further encouragement came through the generosity of the late Jacob Chester Chamberlain, the late Ex-Gov. Daniel Henry Chamberlain, LL. D., and Rev. Leander Trowbridge Chamberlain, D. D., all of New York. By a recent vote of the Chamberlain Association, it was decided to publish the results of these studies of the earlier generations of the descendants of Henry Chamberlin, the earliest of the surname to settle in New England. From the nature of the case, these earlier generations rest in considerable obscurity; and it is the purpose of this genealogical record to set them forth as clearly and as distinctly as can be done after the lapse of two and a half centuries. No person can construct a complete and perfect record of this family, or of any other early New England family. No genealogy has yet been published which is absolutely free from errors. It is most earnestly hoped, however, that this record of the descendants of Henry Chamberlin will not be found upon publication to contain more errors and omissions than the better class of American genealogies contain, and that the time will soon come, when the living descendants of this pioneer, or better the Chamberlain Association, will be disposed to carry forward these generations to a much later period.

FIRST GENERATION

1 HENRY[1] CHAMBERLIN came from Hingham, County of Norfolk, Old England, to New England in the ship *Diligent*, arriving Aug. 10, 1638. With him came his mother Christian, his wife Jane, and two or more children. The time and place of his birth, his baptism and his marriage have not been discovered. That he came to New England from the parish of Hingham cannot be doubted. His relationship to the four or five other Chamberlin families living in that parish from 1600 to 1638 is wholly a matter of conjecture at this time (1907). His mother, Christian Chamberlin, was apparently a widow at the time of her arrival here. She was probably the "Mrs. Chamberlin, widowe, sister to Mr. Israell Stoughton," who received an allowance from Mr. Andrews' gift by the Governor and Deputies of Massachusetts Bay Colony, May 14, 1645. She d. at Hingham, April 19, 1659, æ. 81 years. Hence she must have been b. about 1578. The *Diligent* sailed from Ipswich to London, and from London to New England, bringing not less than 133 passengers who were under the leadership of Rev. Robert Peck, who had been inducted over the parish of Hingham, England, Jan. 7, 1605, and was deposed by Bishop Wren in 1637. The church of St. Andrew, Hingham, was rebuilt in 1316, and still remains a handsome structure with a lofty tower containing eight musical bells. Mr. Peck "fled the kingdom and went over into New England, with many of his parishioners who sold their estates for half their value and conveyed all their effects to that new plantation, erected a town and colonie by the name of Hingham, where many of their posterity are remaining." (Hingham, England, *Parish Register* for 1715.)

Coming to New England to escape religious persecution, Henry Chamberlin was granted land for a house-lot in Hingham, Mass., in 1638. He was admitted a freeman, March 13, 1638-39 (*New England Historic Genealogical Register*, vol. 3, p. 96.) He lived in Hingham from 1638 to 1660, when Feb. 4, 1660, he deeded Daniel Cushing of Hingham, for £3, "all yt my lott containing two acres of upland be it more or lesse as it was given me by ye towne of Hingham, lying and being in ye towneship of Hingham aforesaid in ye field called the Plaine Necke, near unto ye hill called Rocky Hill." (*Suffolk Deeds*, vol. 3, p. 470.) In this and other deeds, he is called a "blacksmith" and a "shoemaker."

"For since the birth of time, throughout all ages and nations,
Has the craft of the smith been held in repute by the people."

He removed across Broad Bay to Hull, a distance of some two or three miles, about 1661, and here he lived until his death, July 15, 1674. Daniel Cushing called him a "shoemaker," and he may have been upon arriving, but from 1660 to his death he styled himself a "blacksmith." He was buried, probably, in the old burying ground on the hill in Hull, but "no man knoweth his sepulchre." "Henry Chamberlin sometime of Hingham but now of Hull in the County of Suffolk in

New England, blacksmith, being weake in body" made his will, Dec. 8, 1673, as follows: To "my loveing wife Jane Chamberlin" her comfortable maintainance; to "my eldest son Henry Chamberlin all my tools belonging to my trade;" to "my two sons Henry Chamberlin and William Chamberlin" equal division of estate; to "my daughter Susan Carter" 20s.; to "my daughter, Ursley Cole," 20s.; to "my daughter Faith Patterson," 20s.; to "my grandchild John Chamberlin," 20s.; joint executors Henry and William Chamberlin his sons; will proved, July 29, 1674. (*Suffolk Probate*, vol. 6, p. 54.) His widow Jane survived her husband, and with her sons gave a joint deed of his house, carpenter houses, lands, and meadow in Hingham to Thomas Sawyer, March 3, 1674-75. (*Suffolk Deeds*, vol. 13, p. 479.) The inventory of his estate shows that he owned land at "Old Planters' Hill" and on the "Plaines" in Hingham. "Chamberlin's Run," a small brook flowing into Wier River, near Rocky Hill, and "Chamberlin's Swamp" beyond Rocky Hill, both in Hingham, perpetuate the name of this pioneer, whose descendants have not dwelt in the ancient town these 200 years.

Children, perhaps not in order:

    i Susannah,[2] b. about 1616; m. before 1649 Joseph Carter of Charlestown and Woburn, Mass. He d. at Charlestown, Jan. 31, 1676–77, æ. 72 years. She m. (2) June 4, 1677, Richard Eccles of Cambridge, Mass. He was a weaver and d. before March 10, 1696–97, she surviving. Her daughter *Susannah*[3] *Carter*, b. about 1649, m. Henry, Summers of Woburn, and d. Oct. 7, 1708, æ. 59 years.

2   ii Henry,[2] eldest son, settled at Hull, Mass.

3 iii William,[2] the Quaker, settled at Hull about 1653.

   iv Daniel,[2] bapt. at Hingham, England, May 15, 1632; buried there, May 19, 1632.

    v Mary,[2] perhaps twin, bapt. at Hingham, England, May 15, 1632; buried there, May 25, 1632.

4 vi John,[2] bapt. at Hingham, England, Nov. 15, 1633.

  vii Ursula,[2] b. about 1634; m. about 1655, John Cole of Charlestown, Mass.; alive in 1673. Their children were: (1) *John*,[3] "mariner;" (2) *Jane*,[3] b. Nov. 1, 1659; alive as Jane Cole, Dec. 2, 1678, when she witnessed Henry[2] Chamberlin's will; (3) and (4) *Martha*[3] and *Ursula*,[3] twins, b. Jan. 25, 1663; Martha[3] d. Feb. 8, 1668. Ursula[3] m. Wigglesworth Sweeter of Boston. (Wyman's *Genealogies of Charlestown*, vol. 1, p. 229.) (5) *James*,[3] who left descendants. She chose Thomas Carter, Sr., and Joseph Carter for her bondsmen, Sept. 6, 1668.

 viii Faith,[2] m. before 1656 Edward Patterson, of Rehoboth from 1643 to 1645; of Hingham in 1652. He was a Quaker, and removed to Freehold, Monmouth County, N. J., as early as 1667. He d. at Freehold before Oct. 5, 1672. She m. (2) between Dec. 8, 1673, and Nov. 6, 1674, Thomas Huet, and witnessed the first recorded Quaker marriage at Shrewsbury, N. J., as "Faith Huet" on 6 d. of 9 mo. 1674. Her children were: (1) *Ralph*[3] *Patterson*, bapt. at Hingham, Mass., Jan. 13, 1655–56, and (2) *Mary*[3] *Patterson*, a witness in Dec., 1688, who m. Ebenezer Cook, and probably others. The mother d. Jan. 30, 1710–11.

  ix Daniel,[2] bapt. at Hingham, Mass., March 17, 1639; no further mention has been found of him.

   x Sarah,[2] bapt. at Hingham, Sept. 26, 1641.

  xi Nathaniel,[2] bapt. at Hingham, Nov. 26, 1643; not mentioned in his father's will in 1673, nor elsewhere.

  xii Ebenezer,[2] probably a son, d. at Hingham, Oct. 28, 1646.

SECOND GENERATION

2 HENRY[2] CHAMBERLIN (*Henry*[1]), called in his father's will "my eldest son," b. probably about 1618; d. at Hull, Mass., Dec. 3, 1678. He was made a freeman in May, 1645. He removed to Hull before 1657 when the proprietors of Hull granted him eight lots in that town, viz. a two acre home-lot in Hull village, a lot at "Allerton Hill" bounded by the "mayne sea" on the east, a lot at "Strait's river," another on Peddock's Island, a fifth at "Strawberry Hill," a sixth at "Sagamore Hill," the seventh at "White Head" and the eighth at "Hogge Island," all in Hull. (*Hull Land Grants*, p. 15.) It appears to me that he was a shoemaker from 1648 to 1672 or longer, and that by assisting his father he acquired the trade of blacksmith, which he certainly followed from 1673 to 1678; townsman, 1661. He m. Sarah Jones who d. at Boston, Dec. 16, 1710, æ. 75 years. She was probably the daughter of Thomas and Ann Jones who came from Southampton in the *Confidence* in 1638. She was b. about 1635. Thomas Jones came from Caversham in Oxfordshire. He d. at Hull, about 1680, and his estate was settled in Essex County, and among his heirs named in March, 1680-81 was "daughter Sarah Chamberlain." In Henry Chamberlin's will made Dec. 2, 1678, he styled himself "by trade Black Smith," "being at this time weake in body," and bequeathed to his wife Sarah with her children "till they come of age," to his daughter Milton £4, "to my other four daughters £6 apiece," "to my two sons Henry Chamberlin and Benjamin Chamberlyn" equal parts except son Henry to have "my Connehasset lott" and "shop tooles for a Smith." Edward Wright and Jane Cole witnessed the will which was probated Jan. 14, 1678-79. The inventory amounted to £270. (*Suffolk Wills*, vol. 6, p. 264, and vol. 12, p. 250.)

Children, perhaps not in order:
  i SARAH,[3] bapt. at Hingham, Mass., June 6, 1652; m. before Dec. 2, 1678, Robert[2] Milton (Joseph[1]) of Hull. He d. at Hull, Nov. 15, 1702. She d. there, July 6, 1719. Their son, *Robert*[3] *Milton, Jr.*, m. Hannah ———— and d. at Hull, May 12, 1722. (Gould MSS.)
  ii JOSEPH,[3] b. about 1653, probably a son. He was a servant to Henry Summers, Jr., of Woburn and was killed while digging a well, Nov. 21, 1670. (*Middlesex Court Files for* 1670.)
5 iii HENRY,[3] joint executor of his father's estate, 1678.
6 iv BENJAMIN,[3] other executor of father's estate, 1678.
  v MARY,[3] m. as second wife, Oct. 13, 1685, Thomas Sawyer of Hingham. She d. before May 21, 1713. Their children were: (1) *Sarah*[4] *Sawyer*, bapt. at Hingham, Oct. 27, 1689; d. soon; (2) *Sarah*[4] *Sawyer*, bapt. August 17, 1690.
  vi JANE,[3] alive and under age, 1678.
  vii ———— a daughter, alive and under age, 1678.
  viii JOANNA,[3] m. in July, 1691, ————.

3 WILLIAM[2] CHAMBERLIN (*Henry*[1]), b. probably about 1620; bought,

Nov. 9, 1647, a house and lot of Francis Smith in Boston situated on the west side of Washington Street between Boylston and West streets and bounded on the west by the "Common." On Jan. 4, 1648, he assigned this lot back to Smith and removed to Hull before Aug. 27, 1654. (*Boston Book of Possessions and Binney MSS.*) He lived on the east side of Quaker Lane in the ancient village of Hull. In 1657 the proprietors of Hull granted and confirmed unto him eleven lots of land in Hull, viz., two lots of six acres in Hull village, a lot at "Peddock's Island," another at "Hogge Island," another at "Strawberry Hill," at "White Head," at "Sagamore Hill," a meadow lot, another at "Lincoln's Rocks," still another at "Huett's Poynt," and confirmed his deed from Thomas Jones of Langley's Island, now a part of the town of Hingham. (*Hull Land Grants*, 1657, p. 43.) He was a selectman about 1658, and was one of the appraisers of Thomas Loring's estate, June 5, 1662; townsman, 1669. He d. at Hull, Oct. 22, 1678, leaving a family of nine children, and an estate valued at £529. He m. first about 1651 a wife, who d. at Hull about 1660. He m. second, about 1661, a wife who was the mother of his four youngest children. The inventory of his estate shows that he took care of his father and mother in their old age. (*Suffolk Wills*, vol. 9, p. 178.)

Children by first wife, probably all born in Hull:
7   i WILLIAM,[3] b. April 9, 1652; lived in Hull.
8   ii JOHN,[3] bapt. at Hingham, Aug. 27, 1654.
9   iii JOB,[3] b. about 1656; removed to Dorchester, S. C.
10 iv NATHANIEL,[3] b. Sept. 4, 1659.
    v FREEDOM,[3] b. about 1660; d. before April 14, 1685, on board of Mr. Condrey's ship which had then arrived at Boston. (*Middlesex Court Files*, 1685.) The inventory of his estate was returned to Middlesex County, Aug. 25, 1685, and his estate was divided among his brothers and half-brothers and half-sisters. (*Middlesex Wills*, vol. 6, p. 346.) At the Suffolk County Court, at the term beginning July 27, 1680, "Freedom Chamberlyn, presented for absenting himselfe from the publique ordinances and frequenting Quakers meetings, being the first conviction, was admonisht and ordered to pay fees of Court."

Children by second wife, all born in Hull:
11 vi BENJAMIN,[3] bapt. at Hingham, May 18, 1662.
12 vii JOSEPH,[3] b. about 1665.
    viii MARY,[3] b. about 1672; d. at Newport, R. I., Oct. 3, 1707. She m. about 1691, Nathaniel Sheffield, a native of Braintree, Mass., who removed to Newport, R. I. He was Deputy from Newport for 1699, 1701, 1702, 1709, 1710, 1711, 1713, and 1718; captain, 1702; general treasurer, 1705 to 1708; inspector of the transcription of the laws of the Colony in 1699; and major of Groat alias Foot Island from 1710 to 1716. He m. (2) Catharine (Gould) Clarke, and d. at Newport, Nov. 12, 1729. Five children.
    ix SARAH,[3] b. about 1676; alive at Newport, in 1693, and then styled a "spinster."

4 JOHN[2] CHAMBERLIN (*Henry*[1]), bapt. at Hingham, County Norfolk, England, Nov. 15, 1633; admitted as an inhabitant of Boston, Mass., July 28, 1651. (*Boston Book of Possessions*, p. 105.) By occupation he was a currier. William Courser of Boston deeded him a dwelling house and lot on Hanover Street,

in Boston, Oct. 14, 1652. (*Suffolk Deeds*, vol. 1, p. 246.) He was present at the execution of Marmaduke Stevenson and William Robinson, and the reprieve of Mary Dyer, on Boston Common, Oct. 27, 1659, and was drawn to visit the Quakers in prison. Witnessing their faith, constancy, and suffering, he became a Quaker, and before Sept. 9, 1661, had been nine times whipped, "three times through three towns." He was imprisoned in Boston, and his father and his brother Henry[2] petitioned the General Court praying for remittance of his "sentence of banishment upon Payne of death," whereupon the Deputies ordered him removed to "Castle Island, there to provide himself lodging, housinge, victualls, etc., at his own charge," etc. The petition was dated June 7, 1661. (*Massachusetts Archives*, vol. 10, p. 272.) About 1663 he removed to Newport, R. I., where he d. about 1667. He m. (1) in Boston, May 19, 1653, Ann or Anna, daughter of William Brown of Boston. She d. soon after his long imprisonment. Of her Bishop wrote in 1702, that "Deputy Governor Bellingham knowing that she was not of the same principle altogether with him, went about to draw her to deny and disown him . . . telling her . . . that when he came home again he would murder her . . .;" that "she should not want and that she might live with another husband." "But being not able to prevail with all his art, on the poor woman who told her true affection to her husband," the "Court . . . could not but order that he should have liberty to work in the prison at his calling which was a currier whereupon he with the help of other Friends rid off his work apace." (Bishop's *New England Judged*, 1702, p. 358, etc.) He m. (2) about 1663, Catherine Chatham, a Quakeress, who came from London to Boston where she "appeared cloathed with sackcloth." She was put in prison, whipped at Dedham, and driven into the wilderness. Imprisoned again and ordered to pay a fine, "she was taken to wife by John Chamberlaine and so became an inhabitant of Boston." (*Ibid*, p. 420.) The will of Nicholas Upsall of Boston, made Aug. 9, 1666, reads, "I Giue my great Coate to the Children of John Chamberlin to cloth them," while his inventory, taken Oct. 31, 1666, referred to the Quakers. (*Register*, vol. 15, p. 251.)

Children by first wife, born in Boston:

 i ANNA,[3] b. Feb. 6, 1653-54.
 ii JOHN,[3] b. May 1, 1655; mentioned in his grandfather's will in 1673; probably erratic; believed to have been the John who d. at Hingham of smallpox, March 28, 1679. His inventory, taken July 11, 1679, amounting to £19 5s. 3d., would seem to indicate that he was a wood-chopper and had no family. He was charged with the robbery of John Coates upon Boston Neck, and was brought into Court May 29, 1673, where he proved that he was in Roxbury at the time of the robbery, but the court sentenced him to pay a fine of 30s. for night walking. At the next session he petitioned from Hull to have his fine remitted, which was granted. (*Suffolk Court Files*.) He was a soldier in King Philip's war, being credited to the town of Hingham, Aug. 24, 1676. (Bodge's *Soldiers in King Philip's War*.)
 iii ELIZABETH,[3] b. Oct. 25, 1656.
13 iv HENRY,[3] b. Feb. 3, 1659; removed to New Jersey.
14 v WILLIAM,[3] b. about 1661; settled in New Jersey.

Children by second wife, born at Newport, Rhode Island:
 vi Susanna,³ b. in Aug., 1664.
15 vii Peleg,³ b. in Aug., 1666; witness at Newport, June 12, 1703.
 viii Jane,³ b. in Dec., 1667; perhaps posthumous.

THIRD GENERATION

5 HENRY³ CHAMBERLIN (*Henry,² Henry¹*), b. at Hull, about 1654; selectman of Hull, 1691, 1694, 1695, 1697; fence viewer, 1683, 1692, 1701, 1704; made oath to the inventory of his father's estate, Jan. 14, 1678-79; received as "an overplus" his father's "Connihasset lott to himselfe for ever and Shop tooles for a Smith." He was a soldier in Capt. Isaac Johnson's Company in Dec., 1675, and was in the great Swamp Fight against King Philip, Dec. 19, 1675. His son John⁴ was a grantee of Narraganset Township No. 5, in 1733. (Bodge's *King Philip's War*.) He was a blacksmith in Hull village, where he d. May 6, 1706. On the day of his death he made his will, "being weake of body," bequeathing to his wife Jane the use of his estate "for ye bringing up of ye children," excepting his shop tools and shop, which he bequeathed to his son Henry⁴ Chamberlin, who was to have a double portion. The will was proved Oct. 2, 1706. (*Suffolk Wills*, vol. 16, p. 182.) The inventory, amounting to £117.18s., included "books and armes £4.12s." He m. about 1682, Jane ———— who survived him and d. after March 16, 1709, and before 1719. "Jane Chamberlin of Hull, widow," for £20, deeded Aaron Pratt of Hingham, yeoman, lot No. 40 in the second division of "Conyhassett uplands in Hingham" March 16, 1709; and six of her children acknowledged that their father gave the lot to their mother, by their deed Oct. 3, 1714. (*Suffolk Deeds*, vol. 36, p. 199.) He was a freeholder of Hull, May 26, 1690.

Children by wife Jane, all born at Hull:
 i Elizabeth,⁴ b. Dec. 20, 1683; alive and unmarried Oct. 3, 1714, when she signed the acknowledgment of her mother's deed as "Elizabeth Chamberlin." The *Gould MSS.* state that she m. Sept. 22, 1709, John Bosworth of Hull, which is probably incorrect as the only John Bosworth named d. Aug. 20, 1693, according to the same MSS.
16 ii Henry,⁴ b. March 11, 1686.
17 iii John,⁴ b. Jan. 29, 1689; alive in Boston, 1733.
 iv Ursula,⁴ b. Jan. 11, 1691; alive and unmarried Oct. 3, 1714; perhaps d. before 1719.
18 v Joseph,⁴ b. April 10, 1694.
19 vi James,⁴ b. March 28, 1697; recorded as the son of Henry and *Elizabeth* Chamberlin on the town records of Hull, but signed with his brothers and sisters as "son of widow Jane Chamberlin of Hull" on Oct. 3, 1714. (*Suffolk Deeds*, vol. 36, p. 199.)
 vii Jane,⁴ b. Dec. 11, 1699; alive Oct. 3, 1714; m. at Hull, Jan. 12, 1719-20, John Oldridge (Aldrich). The intention of marriage of John Eldredge and Jane Chamberlin was entered at Bristol, R. I., in Nov., 1719. (*Vital Records of Rhode Island*, vol. 6, p. 13.) She d. at Bristol, R. I., April 4, 1775, æ. 74 years. He d. there Jan. 29, 1776, æ. 83 years. See *Vital Records of Bristol, R. I.*

6 BENJAMIN³ CHAMBERLIN (*Henry,² Henry¹*), joint executor of his father's estate in 1678, and had a share of his father's estate.

What became of this Benjamin Chamberlin and of his Hull property is unknown, as no records of him and it have been found after diligent search. Possibly the Court Files of Suffolk County may show. Probably he was a mariner and d. unmarried.

7 WILLIAM³ CHAMBERLIN (*William,² Henry¹*), b. at Hingham, or Hull, April 9, 1652; d. at Hull, Dec. 11, 1709. He was a weaver and a Quaker, and lived in the old Chamberlin homestead in Quaker Lane in ancient Hull village. He was a soldier in King Philip's war, and served in Capt. Isaac Johnson's Company in Dec., 1675. He was, probably, with his company in the Great Swamp Fight Dec. 19, 1675. (Bodge's *Soldiers in King Philip's War.*) He was m. at the house of Joseph Coleman in Scituate, according to Quaker custom, Nov. 9, 1678, to Eunice Ewell, daughter of Henry Ewell of Scituate. By order of the Superior Court, Jan. 28, 1678-79, he was apportioned £100 of his father's estate, "hee defaulting thereout the value of the Land his ffather gave him before his death," and on April 29, 1679, he was appointed guardian unto "Nathaniel, Mary, and Benjamin Chamberlyn, three of the children of William Chamberlyn, late of Hull, deceased." In the settlement of his father's estate, it was agreed that he should "have the new house in Hull and the old barne" with "halfe the land belonging to both houses," "provided he pay unto his brothers, Nathaniel and Benjamin, and to his sister Mary, when they become of age, £50 apiece, and teach all the children to read and write." He and his wife Eunice deeded the new end of their house, formerly belonging to their father, to Elizabeth Phippeny of Hull, widow, Dec. 18, 1708. (*Suffolk Deeds*, vol. 24, p. 175.) He was a freeholder of Hull, May 26, 1690.

He was a trustee of the Quaker Meetinghouse in Boston in 1695, which occupied the site of the "Quincy House" of 1875. The deed conveying this property to the trustees read, "to the only sole and proper use for the service and worship of Almighty God by the Society or comunity of People called Quakers," and was dated Feb. 2, 1695. (*Binney MSS.*) He was a lighterman at Hull in 1698.

Children by wife Eunice, all born in Hull:

20 i EBENEZER,⁴ b. Nov. 8, 1679; sea-captain from Boston.
21 ii WILLIAM,⁴ b. Jan. 24, 1681.
  iii HOPE,⁴ b. Feb. 22, 1683; m. in 1711, Samuel James of Hingham, Mass. He d. at Hingham, Aug. 20, 1749, æ. 73 years.
  iv MARCY,⁴ b. Nov. 18, 1686; int. m. at Boston, June 9, 1714, with Isaac Anthony; alive March 23, 1729, and called "Mercy Anthony."
  v PRESERVE,⁴ b. June 3, 1692; bequeathed £10 by the disallowed will of her brother, Ebenezer⁴ Chamberlin, March 29, 1729. (*Suffolk Wills*, vol. 27, p. 514.)
22 vi SAMUEL,⁴ b. Dec. 27, 1694.
23 vii JOB,⁴ b. Oct. 27, 1697.

8 JOHN³ CHAMBERLIN (*William,² Henry¹*), bapt. at Hingham, Aug. 27,

1654, when his father was described as "of Hull." He m. before April 3, 1678, Deborah, daughter of Richard and Hannah, or Anna, (Pritchard) Templar of Yarmouth and of Charlestown, Mass. Her father d. before 1674, and her mother Anna m. (2) April 29, 1674, Nathaniel Morton of Plymouth, Secretary of Plymouth Colony from 1645 to 1685, and author of *New England's Memorial*. Deborah Templar was b. at Yarmouth, Oct. 4, 1657. He was a cordwainer and a constable in Charlestown, where he assisted in deposing Sir Edmund Andros. He d. at Charlestown of smallpox, Dec. 22, 1690. His wife's mother, Anna Morton, d. there also, Dec. 26, 1690, "an aged widow." His widow, Deborah Chamberlin, m. (2) at Charlestown, Aug. 13, 1691, Abraham Miller, and d. before April 12, 1693, when the inventory of her estate was taken. (*Middlesex Probate Files*, 2779.) Nathaniel Morton and his wife Anne of New Plymouth, for good will "that they bear unto their loving son-in-law, John Chamberline of Charlestown, cordwainer," deeded him the southerly end of their house in Charlestown, then occupied by him, June 30, 1680. (*Middlesex Deeds*, vol. 8, p. 379.) His wife received a legacy of £10 from her grandfather, Richard Pritchard, April 3, 1678. (*Ibid*, vol. 7, p. 81.) Administration upon the estate of John Chamberlin was granted to Job Chamberlin of Boston and Henry Summers of Woburn in 1691. His inventory was taken June 16, 1691.

Children born at Charlestown, except the first:
  i John,[4] b. at Hull, Jan. 30, 1678-79, bapt. at Charlestown, May 14, 1682; d. there July 24, 1684, æ. 5 years.
  ii Hannah,[4] b. Aug. 2, 1681, bapt. May 14, 1682; living unmarried at Charlestown, Nov. 30, 1705.
  iii Mary,[4] b. Oct. 10, bapt. 14, 1683; m. in Boston, Aug. 31, 1704, Ebenezer Tolman, a tailor of Boston.
  iv Deborah,[4] b. June 27, bapt. July 3, 1687; living at Woburn, Nov. 30, 1705. (*Middlesex Deeds*, vol. 14, p. 99.)
  v Sarah,[4] b. Jan. 15, bapt. 19, 1689; m. (1) in Boston, Jan. 24, 1705-6, Josiah, son of Nathaniel Clark. He was b. at Newbury, May 7, 1682; d. in Boston, April 29, 1717. She m. (2) May 26, 1720, Joseph Woodwell of Bridgewater, Cotton Mather performing the ceremony. Children: (1) *John*[5] *Clark*, b. Oct. 21, 1710; (2) *Josiah*[5] *Clark*, b. Jan. 1, 1713.

As all descendants are of other names no further record will be given of this family.

9 JOB[3] CHAMBERLIN (*William*,[2] *Henry*[1]), b. at Hull, Mass., about 1656; m. about 1684, Joanna Way, daughter of Aaron and Joanna (Sumner) Way of Rumney Marsh (now Chelsea), Mass. She was b. at Rumney Marsh, March 5, 1663. Her father made his will Aug. 25, 1695, bequeathing "to my daughter Joanna, or to her children in case she dies before it is paid." His will was proved, Sept. 20, 1695. Soon after the widow, Joanna Way, her two brothers, and Job Chamberlin and his family, all under the leadership of Rev. Joseph Lord of Dorchester and Elder William Pratt of Weymouth, removed from Boston to Dorchester on the Ashley River, near Charleston, in South Carolina.

Job[3] Chamberlin was a shipwright, living at Hull in 1686; he removed to

Scituate, then to Boston, and about 1696 or 1697 to Dorchester, S. C. March 5, 1685-86, he sold for £7 "unto my Brother William Chamberlin of Hull, weaver, that lot which was our father William Chamberlin's." His wife Joanna signed this deed with him. (*Suffolk Deeds*, vol. 44, p. 183.) On May 10, 1723, he gave the power of attorney to Ebenezer Chamberlin of Boston to sell land in Hull, when he was described as a "shipwright of South Carolina." (*Suffolk Deeds*, vol. 84, p. 141.) After removing to Dorchester, S. C., they requested and received letters of dismissal and recommendation from Increase Mather and Cotton Mather, pastors of the Second Church of Boston, dated Oct. 31, 1698. He owned a lot in the second division of Dorchester, S. C., in 1702. (*South Carolina Historical and Genealogical Magazine*, vol. 6, p. 74.)

Children born and baptized in Boston:
24 i Job,[4] b. May 16, 1685, bapt. Feb. 23, 1690.
25 ii William,[4] b. Jan. 16, 1687, bapt. Feb. 23, 1690.
    iii Elizabeth,[4] b. Jan. 11, 1688-89, bapt. Feb. 23, 1690.
    iv Aaron,[4] b. Jan. 7, 1691; d. in Boston, Feb. 13, 1691.
    v Moses,[4] twin, b. Jan. 7, 1691; d. in Boston, Feb. 5, 1691.
    vi Susannah,[4] b. Nov. 23, bapt. 26, 1693.
    vii Mary,[4] b. Nov. 30, bapt. Dec. 8, 1695.

Possibly others were born in South Carolina, although no record of such has yet been found.

10 NATHANIEL[3] CHAMBERLIN (*William*,[2] *Henry*[1]), was b. at Hull, Mass., Sept. 4, 1659; m. probably in Quaker meeting at Scituate, Mass., Sept. 19, 1681, Abigail Rogers, daughter of John Rogers, Jr., by his second wife Elizabeth. She was b. at Marshfield, Mass., Nov. 3, 1663. He lived in Scituate from 1681 to 1690; in Hull from 1690 to 1695; removed to Scituate in 1695, or to that part of the ancient town which was set off as Pembroke in 1712. At any rate he lived in Pembroke from 1712 until his death there Sept. 22, 1716. His wife Abigail survived him. He was a weaver and a husbandman, and he and his wife were both members of the Friends, or Quaker society in Scituate and Pembroke. The births of his first eight children are recorded on the Scituate Friends' Records, and these and four others are also recorded on the Hull town records. In the probate of his estate at Plymouth, four others are named, making sixteen children. The Scituate Friends' records show that on Aug. 31, 1690, he was "about to remove to Hull." Upon the incorporation of Pembroke, March 21, 1712, his family consisted of seventeen persons. He purchased land in Scituate (perhaps now Pembroke, or Hanson), Oct. 25, 1697. Nathaniel Chamberlin, "late of Hull and now of Scituate, weaver," and Abigail his wife, for £24, deeded William Chamberlin of Hull, weaver, our rights in the old house and land in Hull, Oct. 6, 1698. (*Suffolk Deeds*, vol. 44, p. 183.) In the settlement of his estate mention is made of his sons Nathaniel, Benjamin, and Joseph, his widow Abigail, his daughters Eunice and Patience, and "the son of Ruth Fletcher, deceased, grandson of said Nathaniel, deceased." The inventory mentioned his "farme" and buildings, valued at £200,

and "lands near the division between Duxborrough and Pembroke," and "lands in the cedar swamp." (*Plymouth Probate*, vol. 3, p. 446, and vol. 4, p. 259.) His widow Abigail's dower was set off to her in 1721. Edward Wanton of Scituate, the Quaker minister, bequeathed to him and his two daughters, Abigail and Joanna Chamberlin, in his will in 1716. Joanna Butler, a daughter of John Rogers, Jr., gave legacies to her cousins, Elizabeth Chamberlin and Patience Chamberlin, Dec. 6, 1745.

Children, first eight born in Scituate, next four in Hull, and last four in Pembroke:
  i ELIZABETH,⁴ b. June 18, 1682; alive and unmarried, Dec. 6, 1745.
26 ii NATHANIEL,⁴ b. Aug. 13, 1683.
27 iii JOHN,⁴ b. Dec. 26, 1684.
  iv MARY,⁴ b. Feb. 5, 1685-86.
  v JOANNA,⁴ b. Jan. 17, 1686-87; alive and unmarried in 1716.
  vi ABIGAIL,⁴ b. Feb. 28, 1687-88; m. at Pembroke, Feb. 2, 1726, Jonathan Boyce of Salem, Mass.
  vii SARAH,⁴ b. April 8, 1689; d. Sept. 9, 1689.
  viii PATIENCE,⁴ b. April 28, 1690; alive and unmarried, Dec. 6, 1745.
  ix BATHSHEBA,⁴ b. June 28, 1692.
  x EXPERIENCE,⁴ twin, b. June 28, 1692.
  xi RUTH,⁴ b. Dec. 1, 1693; m. at Pembroke, April 28, 1719, John Fletcher of Harwick (now Brewster), Mass. She d. probably before 1721, leaving one son.
28 xii THOMAS,⁴ b. May 21, 1695.
29 xiii FREEDOM,⁴ b. about 1697; settled in Pembroke.
  xiv EUNICE,⁴ b. about 1698; alive in 1716.
30 xv JOSEPH,⁴ b. about 1699.
  xvi BENJAMIN,⁴ youngest son, b. about 1700. He d. before April 18, 1724. His nuncupative will was dated March 6, 1723-24, in which he provided that his mother, his sisters Eunice and Patience, and his brother Joseph should have a living out of his estate; to his "cousin Naomi who had been sick a great while" he gave £10, to pay "ye Doctor," and to his sisters Abigail and Joanna he gave £12 each. His brother Freedom⁴ Chamberlin of Pembroke was appointed administrator, April 18, 1724. He probably d. unmarried.

11 BENJAMIN³ CHAMBERLIN (*William*,² *Henry* ¹), b. at Hull about 1662; bapt. at Hingham, May 18, 1662; m. at Hingham, Oct. 13, 1685, Mary, daughter of Edward Wright of Scituate. He was living at Hull in 1686, after which no further trace of him has been found there. No record of any transfer of property is found in Suffolk County in his name. Probably he removed from the locality, although he witnessed a Quaker marriage at Scituate, Feb. 12, 1702-3.

Child born at Hull:
31 i BENJAMIN, b. July 28, 1686.

12 JOSEPH³ CHAMBERLIN (*William*,² *Henry* ¹), b. at Hull about 1665. William James of Scituate was his guardian in 1685. "Joseph Chamberlin of Hull, cordwainer," for £12, deeded "my brother William Chamberlin of Hul,

weaver, land on Pettox Island which was our father William Chamberlin's and afterwards our brother Freedom Chamberlin's and now mine," March 30, 1687. (*Suffolk Deeds*, vol. 44, p. 181.) He removed to Hadley, Mass., about 1688, and to Hatfield before 1701; from Hadley or Hatfield, Mass., he removed to Colchester, Conn., as early as 1704. Joseph Chamberlin of Hadley executed at Hatfield, May 29, 1693, a power of attorney unto his brother William Chamberlin of Hull. (*Suffolk Deeds*, vol. 17, p. 15.) Mercy Chamberlin, his wife, quitclaimed all interest in her husband's estate at Hull unto Nathaniel Chamberlin, weaver, and John Collier, husbandman, both of Hull, May 31, 1695. (*Suffolk Deeds*, vol. 17, p. 131.) He was a petit juror at Hadley in 1701, and his taxes were referred to at Hadley and Hatfield in 1703. (Colonel Harding's *Chamberlain Genealogical Record*, p. 9.) The earliest mention of him at Colchester was April 1, 1703, when the proprietors of Colchester "granted to Thomas Day the lott that was formerly granted to Joseph Chamberlin," and Oct. 30, 1704, they "further granted unto Joseph Chamberlin twenty acres of upland for his meadow if it be on Wigwam Hill" with a £200 right. Proof is wanting to show that he ever lived in Weathersfield, Conn., as Stiles stated. (*History of Wethersfield*, vol. 2, p. 205.) From 1704 until his death he was a prominent man in Colchester. He was a selectman in Colchester in 1705, 1706, 1716–18, and perhaps other years. In 1710 he was licensed to keep an "ordynary," and he continued to keep a tavern from 1710 to 1748. The Governor and Council of Connecticut ordered the treasurer to pay him £1.13s. for entertaining the French ambassadors when they passed through Colchester to and from New London in March, 1711. (*Colonial Records of Connecticut*, vol. 5, p. 305.) In 1714 he presented a bill of 14s. 5d. for Lieutenant Crocker's expenses. He was made a freeman, Dec. 31, 1712. He lived on the main road leading from New London to Hartford, and about one mile north of the present village of Colchester. He was a large landowner in Colchester, and about 1741 sold large portions of his estate "for parental love and good will" unto his sons. He m. at Hadley, Mass., June 8, 1688, Mercy Dickinson, daughter of John and Frances (Foote) Dickinson. She was b. at Wethersfield, Conn., about 1668, and d. at Colchester, June 30, 1735, "in ye 67th year of her age." He d. at Colchester, Aug. 7, 1752, æ. 87 years, and was buried in the old parish cemetery in Colchester village.

Children perhaps not all in order:

32   i WILLIAM,[1] b. about 1689; lived in Colchester.
  ii SARAH,[4] b. at Hadley, Nov. 2, 1690; d. there, Jan. 27, 1691.
  iii SARAH,[4] b. at Hadley, March 10, 1693; m. at Colchester, Conn., in June, 1708, Ephraim Foote, son of Nathaniel and Margaret (Bliss) Foote of Hatfield and Springfield, Mass., and of Stratford, Branford, and Wethersfield, Conn. He was b. at Wethersfield, Feb. 13, 1685, and d. June 10, 1765, æ. 80. She d. June 9, 1777, æ. 84. For nine children see *Foote Family*, p. 51.
  iv ELIZABETH,[4] b. about 1695; m. at Colchester, Sept. 8, 1715, John Wells (Welles), son of Noah and Sarah (Wyatt) Welles of Colchester, and had *Mary*[5] *Wells*, b. July 15, 1716, and *John*[5] *Wells*, b. Nov. 24, 1718.

33   v   JOSEPH,⁴ b. about 1697; settled in Colchester.
    vi   JOHN,⁴ b. at Hatfield, Mass., March 4, 1700; probably d. soon.
34 vii   BENJAMIN,⁴ b. about 1701; lived in Colchester.
35 viii   FREEDOM,⁴ b. at Colchester, April 15, 1705.
36 ix   JOHN,⁴ b. at Colchester, Jan. 31, 1707-8.

13 HENRY³ CHAMBERLIN (*John*,² *Henry*¹), b. in Boston, Feb. 3, 1659; removed with his parents to Newport, R. I., about 1663. "Henry Chamberlin, eldest son of John Chamberlin, deceased, of Rhode Island," deeded Valentine Huddlestone of Newport, all interest in his father's estate in Rhode Island, March 20, 1680. (*Newport Deeds*.) He removed to Shrewsbury, N. J., before March 25, 1687. He d. at Manesquam, or Manasquan (perhaps Squankum) Monmouth County, N. J., before Feb. 14, 1688-89, upon which date his widow, Anne Chamberlin, returned the inventory of his estate, and Feb. 15, 1688-89, she was appointed administratrix of the estate of Henry Chamberline of "Shrosberry." He m. Anne, whose surname was Laffetra or West, daughter, or step-daughter, of Edmond and Frances Laffetra. She made her will Jan. 15, 1691-92, and it was proved Jan. 25, 1691-92. She mentioned her brothers Robert and Joseph West, her son John Chamberlin then under age, and her mother and sisters, whose names were not given. Joseph West was commissioned executor, Dec. 29, 1692. (*New Jersey Wills*, Book E, p. 9.)

Child:
37   JOHN,⁴ b. about 1679; settled in Shrewsbury.

14 WILLIAM³ CHAMBERLIN (*John*,² *Henry*¹), b. in Boston about 1661; witnessed Henry Chamberlin's deed to Valentine Huddlestone of Newport, March 20, 1680. He removed to Shrewsbury, N. J., before 1687. He was a "cooper," and deeded his right in one-half of a patent of 100 acres to Edward Woolley of Shrewsbury, Nov. 19, 1687. (*New Jersey Deeds*, Book B, p. 301.) He d. before July 8, 1717, when John Chamberlin was appointed guardian of his son Henry, at which time he was "deceased." (*New Jersey Wills*, Book A, p. 51.) He m. ——————, a daughter of Nathaniel Raulins of Elizabeth, N. J., who made his will, Oct. 10, 1691.

Child:
38 i HENRY,⁴ b. between 1695 and 1704.

15 PELEG³ CHAMBERLIN (*John*,² *Henry*¹), b. at Newport, R. I., in Aug., 1666; witnessed the deed from Capt. Nathaniel Sheffield of Newport to William Chamberlin of Hull, Mass., weaver, June 12, 1703. (*Suffolk Deeds*, vol. 44, p. 182.) He m. Susanna ———— who was b. about 1668, and d. at Newport, R. I., Jan. 8, 1721-22, æ. 53 years. She was buried in the Clifton graveyard. He, or his son of the same name, was admitted a freeman of the colony, May 6, 1707. No further record has been found.

Children, possibly born to the foregoing:
i PELEG,[4] freeman of Rhode Island, May 6, 1707.
ii JOSEPH,[4] freeman of the colony, May 6, 1707, when his surname was written Chanterlin, which was possibly intended for Chamberlin. Also written on Newport records Joseph Chantrell, which throws much doubt upon the identification.
iii EBENEZER,[4] possibly a son, lived at Bristol, R. I., but d. at Cape Breton, Dec. 31, 1746. His wife was probably the Mrs. Chamberlin who d. at Bristol, Feb. 22, 1737.

A CHAMBERLAIN GENEALOGICAL RECORD

By Colonel William J. Harding

[Colonel Harding has kindly permitted the Association to reproduce, as a supplement to the preceding article, certain portions of a pamphlet privately printed for his family's use. It contains biographical and genealogical sketches of the Chamberlain ancestors of Mrs. Harding. The line of descent is: Henry [1] Chamberlin (1596-1674) of Hingham and Hull, Mass.; William [2] (died 1678) of Hull: Joseph [3] (1665-1752) of Hull and Hadley, Mass., and Colchester, Conn.; William [4] (1688-89-1756) of Colchester; Peleg [5] (1713———) of Colchester and Kent, Conn.; Peleg [6] (1736-1808) of Kent and New Milford, Conn.; Swift [7] (1764-1828) of Kent, Conn., and Monkton, Vt.; Hiram [8] (1797-1866) of Monkton, Vt., and Brownsville, Texas; Adelia [9] Chamberlain, wife of Col. Wm. J. Harding of Brooklyn, N. Y. As the three earliest generations are described in the preceding article, they will be omitted here, and the sketches given below will begin with the fourth generation,—William Chamberlain of Colchester, Conn. As Colonel Harding's description of his search for his wife's ancestors during his leisure moments from December, 1897 to December, 1906, may assist and encourage others to trace their ancestry, the preface to his pamphlet is included.]

WHEN I undertook the tracing of my wife's ancestry on her father's side, little was known in her family on the subject, beyond the fact that her father, Hiram Chamberlain, was born at Monkton, Vt.: that he was educated at Middlebury College, Vt., and at the theological seminaries at Andover, Mass., and Princeton, N. J., and in early life had been ordained by the New York Presbytery. Even the Christian name and place of birth of Mr. Chamberlain's father was not known to them, nor the name of his mother. Mr. Chamberlain's pastorate duties took him into the Southern States immediately after his ordination in 1825. He was twice married before 1842, but of these marriages only one child, a daughter of the first marriage, attained maturity and survived her father. There was no issue of the second marriage. The last sixteen years of Mr. Chamberlain's life (1850-66) were spent at Brownsville, Tex., and there the children of his third marriage were brought up or born, strangers to their father's old home, and remembered but little about their relatives in far away New England, except that their father had a brother, named Peleg, and other relatives with whom he sometimes corresponded. The total destruction, soon after Mr. Chamberlain's death, of the family residence at Brownsville with all its contents, including Mr. Chamberlain's papers, correspondence, and books, during the terrible tornado of 1867, completely closed all avenues of information, excepting such general and imperfect recollections of what from time to time may have fallen from Mr. Chamberlain's own lips with reference to his kindred.

Accordingly the first step taken was to communicate with the college authorities and examine the general catalogues of Middlebury, Andover, and Princeton; but these yielded no information concerning Mr. Chamberlain's parentage. Correspondence was then opened with a Vermont lawyer, practicing in the vicinity of Monkton, and the interest and help of my wife's younger brother, Mr. Edwin Chamberlain of San Antonio, Tex., was enlisted in the subject. By the end of January, 1898, Mr. Edwin Chamberlain and I, from different sources, learned that there were gravestones in Monkton cemetery which bore the names of Swift Chamberlain, who died in 1828, and of his wife Mary, who died in 1858. About the same time a helpful fact was gleaned from the *Tuttle Family Genealogy*, viz., that "Polly, daughter of Thomas Tuttle, married ———— Chamberlain of Monkton, Addison County, Vt., and had a large family, of whom a daughter married Ryland Doughten." The additional fact that Ryland Doughten was dead, and that Emily Doughten had lived at Monkton, with Swift Chamberlain's widow, was clearly of value. From these isolated facts, taken together, the inference was drawn that Mrs. Harding's grandfather and grandmother were Swift Chamberlain and Mary Tuttle; and on this assumption the investigation was continued; but with the supposition that the Chamberlains were of Vermont. The unusual Christian name "Swift," suggesting a maternal surname, was of peculiar value in instituting further researches, as will be seen later on.

Correspondence was then carried on with various persons who were supposed to be possessed of facts which would be helpful; but this method was abandoned after it had been prosecuted for several years without substantial results.

In 1902 I secured the assistance of Mr. Eben Putnam of Boston, an experienced and skillful genealogist, and, guided by his patient and intelligent investigations, the facts which led to final success were slowly brought to light. Mr. Putnam at once expressed doubts of the value of the tradition that Mr. Chamberlain's ancestors had quite recently come from England, and settled at Montpelier, Vt.; and favored a Massachusetts origin of the family. None of Mr. Putnam's Chamberlain "notes" showed a Swift Chamberlain; nor did Ellery's *Genealogy of the Swift Family* disclose a marriage with a Chamberlain. Upon examining the Connecticut Revolutionary War records, it was found that a Swift Chamberlain and a Peleg Chamberlain of Kent, in western Connecticut, were Revolutionary soldiers. The finding of these significant names was decidedly encouraging; moreover, further research showed that a Peleg Chamberlain married, Oct. 4, 1759, Abigail Swift of Sandwich, Mass., at Kent, Conn., which indicated how Swift Chamberlain came by his Christian name—assuming that Peleg and Swift were father and son.

The next discovery was that a John Chamberlain, born 1626, of Newport, had a son Peleg, born 1666, and that a Peleg Chamberlain was admitted freeman at Newport in 1707. Much time was spent in endeavoring to connect this Newport Peleg with our Kent Peleg, but unsuccessfully, although the necessary researches brought out much that was interesting and ultimately valuable, including the fact that John was a son of Henry of Hingham. The difficulty was increased by the condition of the Newport records, examination of the most important of which being forbidden on account of their condition, these records having suffered greatly during the Revolutionary War.

A critical point in the investigation had now been reached. About this time, viz., May, 1903, vol. 9 of the *Collections of the Connecticut Historical Society* was issued, giving names of French and Indian War soldiers from Connecticut; and, to our great joy, was found to contain the names of a Peleg Chamberlain of Colchester and a Peleg, Jr., of Kent. It was also found that when the development of the town of Kent was begun in 1739, several persons of the name of Swift from Sandwich, Mass., and many people from Colchester, and Hebron, became interested in the place.

The Colchester records, being in print, showed that a William Chamberlain, born 1689, had a son Peleg, born 1713. Here evidently was our clue.

On further search it was found that there were at least two distinct families of Chamberlain at Colchester; one, descended from Richard of Braintree: the other represented by a Joseph Chamberlain, who, it was thought, might be descended from Henry of Hingham. This Joseph had apparently settled in Colchester about 1704, and it was soon found, from the Colchester deeds, that William, born 1689, was the son of this Joseph, and the father of Peleg, Sr.

Thus it became possible to construct the following tentative pedigree: JOSEPH CHAMBERLAIN of Colchester, WILLIAM of Colchester, born 1689, PELEG of Colchester, born 1713, PELEG of Colchester and Kent, married Abigail Swift, SWIFT of Kent, died 1828 at Monkton, Vt., married Mary (Tuttle?), HIRAM, born 1797 at Monkton, Vt.

From the records of Hingham and Hull, Mass., and the probate and other records of Suffolk County, Mass., it appeared that William Chamberlain of Hull, son of Henry of Hingham, the immigrant of 1638, had a son named Joseph and another son named Freedom. This Joseph was traced to Hadley, where he married Mercy Dickinson, and then to Hatfield, but no record of him there after about 1687 was found. As this Joseph of Hadley and the Joseph of Colchester were apparently about the same age, the former with a brother Freedom, the latter with a son Freedom, it was felt sure that they were one and the same person. I would not, however, take this for granted, but continued the investigation.

After much persistent labor, Mr. Putnam's skill was rewarded by discovering at Springfield, Mass., the records of a series of litigation which established the fact beyond question, that Joseph of Colchester was he of Hadley, and a grandson of Henry of Hingham. This completed the line from Henry Chamberlain the immigrant of 1638 to my wife.

All other details, with dates of marriages, births, and deaths, names and pedigrees of the wives, information from wills, deeds, church records, etc., were gradually looked up and added from time to time.

Much difficulty was, however, experienced in establishing the identity of Mary, Swift Chamberlain's wife, and in determining whether she or a former wife was the mother of Mr. Hiram Chamberlain.

The Monkton records of the birth of ten of the children of Swift and Mary, or Polly, Chamberlain began with April, 1799, and, of course, made no mention of Hiram, who was born in 1797. Examination of the marriage and other records of Monkton and near-by towns, and of the recorded deeds and probate proceedings in Addison and adjoining counties of Vermont, failed to disclose the sought-for information, although much that was interesting concerning the Chamberlain and Tuttle families was met with.

Finally, late in 1906, the question was determined through the United States Pension Records of the Revolutionary War, which gave the date and place of marriage of Swift Chamberlain and Mary Tuttle.

Of all that is set forth in the following pages there is ample proof which would be received and accepted as evidence in any court of law or equity.

The list of authorities consulted and examined will give some idea of the scope and extent of the investigation which was necessary to bring about a successful result.

WILLIAM CHAMBERLAIN, 1688-89-1756

WILLIAM CHAMBERLAIN, son of Joseph Chamberlain of Hadley and Colchester and his wife Mercy Dickinson, and probably the eldest son, was born at Hadley in the year 1688-89, perhaps in March, which would make him 67 at his death in 1756. He doubtless went to Colchester in 1704 or 1705 with his father. Besides the mansion house and home-lot at Colchester, the gift of his father, he had a home-lot which he bought of Joseph Dewey in 1712, just after his marriage. That he owned real and personal property both at Colchester and Hebron, appears from his son Peleg's deed of quitclaim (mentioned below), to the other children, made in 1757. He was appointed administrator of his father's estate, March 11, 1756, at which time he apparently was "of Hebron," but no settlement of the estate has been traced. He died Oct. 31, 1756, aged 67, according to the record on his gravestone, which must be correct—rather than 1755, as given in the town record—in view of the date of the letters of administration upon his father's estate.

William Chamberlain was married at Colchester, Jan. 4, 1710-11, to Sarah Day, who survived him and was living in 1757. His children, twelve in number, were as follows: William, born at Colchester, Jan. 22, 1711-12; PELEG, of whom below; John, born Jan. 10, 1716, and Sarah, Mercy, and Mary, no date. The names of the above-mentioned six children appear in the town records of Colchester and also in the deed from Peleg to his brothers and sisters, dated Feb. 8, 1757, acknowledged the same day at Glastonbury, whereby, for divers good causes, and in consideration of two hundred pounds, he quitclaimed to his brothers and sisters, naming them, "all my share in real and personal estate of my honored father William Chamberlain, late of Colchester, both in Colchester and Hebron: also any estate which may descend to me from my honored mother Sarah Chamberlain after her decease." In this quitclaim deed Sarah is described as Sarah Foote,

Mercy as Mercy Ward, and Mary as Mary Foote. Three other children, viz., Nathaniel, Ebenezer, and Joel were also named in Peleg's quitclaim. Nathaniel was born Sept. 24, 1722, and, it is said, married Deliverance, daughter of Thomas Snell. The three remaining children, Rhoda, Elizabeth and Meriam, are described in Peleg's quitclaim as Rhoda Worthington, Elizabeth Jones, and Meriam Scovell.

AUTHORITIES

Hadley Town Records.
Colchester Deeds, vol. 1, p. 339, 2, p. 90, 5, p. 327.
Gravestone of William Chamberlain at Colchester.
Colchester Records, vol. 2, p. 445.
East Haddam Records.
Chamberlain Association Report, 1902, p. 30.

Colchester was originally a part of Hartford County and remained so until 1741, after which and until 1832 it was of East Haddam. Probate must be looked for at Hartford, East Haddam, and Colchester.

PELEG CHAMBERLAIN, 1713

PELEG CHAMBERLAIN, son of William Chamberlain of Colchester and Hebron and Sarah Day his wife, was born at Colchester, Nov. 25, 1713, and died at Kent, Conn., after 1766, the year being uncertain. In 1743, Jan. 30, he was received into the membership of the First Church at Colchester, his wife, Experience, having been similarly admitted May 16, 1742. In a deed to him dated Dec. 5, 1753, from Charles Buckley, of several lots of land in Kent, Conn., 117 acres in all, he is described as of Colchester. Between the latter date and July, 1754, he must have removed to Kent, for William, the first child of his second marriage, was born at Kent in that month, and in a quitclaim deed of Feb. 8, 1757, to his brothers and sisters, he is described as "of Kent." On Feb. 18, 1758, he was admitted to full communion in the Church at Kent on recommendation of the Church at Colchester; and his wife, Jane, was similarly admitted in 1764. He and his wife Jane appear on the list of members of the Church at Kent in 1766. Peleg Chamberlain was a soldier from Connecticut in the French and Indian War, and enlisted in the 7th or Capt. Ichabod Phelps' Company of the 3d, or Col. Eliphalet Dyer's Regiment, Sept. 6, 1755, and was discharged Nov. 25, 1755. He re-enlisted the same day, and was assigned to the 3d, or Major Payson's, Company of Col. Jonathan Bagley's Regiment, and was discharged from the same company, then commanded by Capt. Noah Grant (grandfather of Gen. U. S. Grant), May 21, 1756.

Peleg Chamberlain was married twice, as follows: First, at Colchester, May 8, 1735, to Experience Bartlett, who died March 21, 1748-49, aged 39, sixteen days after the birth of Experience, her only daughter. Second, at Colchester, Jan. 16, 1752, to Jane Higgins, who was living at Kent in 1766.

His children were as follows: Of his first marriage, all of whom were born at Colchester, PELEG, of whom below; Eleazer, born Aug. 14, 1737, married at Kent, March 8, 1759, to Eleanor Pratt, and died March 25, 1805; Nathan, baptized Oct. 28, 1739, died April 6, 1740; Nathan, baptized April 19, 1741, and was living in 1794; Samuel, born Sept. 9, 1743, baptized Oct. 16, 1743; Jonathan, born Feb. 3, 1745-46, baptized March 30, 1746, and believed to have died at Austerlitz, Columbia County, N. Y.; Experience, born March 5, 1748-49, baptized March 30, 1749, married Mr. Spencer and settled in Spencertown, N. Y. Of his second marriage: William, born at Kent, July 26, 1754; Elizabeth, born at Kent, Aug. 1, 1762, baptized Sept. 19, 1762, married Richard Peck and died May 4, 1838. In addition, Peleg is said to have had Elisha, Benjamin, Louis H., John, and Sarah. Peleg, Jr., Eleazer, Samuel, William, and (perhaps) Elisha were soldiers from Connecticut in the Revolutionary War.

AUTHORITIES

Colchester Records.
Records of the First Church at Colchester. Copy in possession of the Chamberlain Association.
Records of church at Kent.
Kent Deeds, vol. 11, p. 110.
Atwater's *History of Kent*, 1897.
Collections Connecticut Historical Society, vol. 9, pp. 34, 42, 76, 77, 86, 87.
Collection of Epitaphs by F. E. Randall.
Experience Chamberlain's Gravestone, Colchester Village.
Nathan Chamberlain's Gravestone, Colchester Village.
Chamberlain Association Reports, 1902.
Connecticut Men in the Revolution.
Peck Genealogy.
Letter of Geo. W. Chamberlain.

The Town of Kent was laid out in 1710, but no further steps regarding its settlement were taken until 1737. In 1738 the township was sold at public auction in Windham, by the colony, and was bought by Humphrey Avery of Groton, who represented a company.

PELEG CHAMBERLAIN, 1736-1808

PELEG CHAMBERLAIN, eldest son of Peleg Chamberlain of Colchester and Kent, and Experience Bartlett his wife, was born at Colchester, May 12, 1736, was baptized June 20, 1736, and died at New Milford, Conn., after June 7, 1808, that being the date of his will. About 1753 or 1754 his father removed from Colchester to Kent. During the French and Indian War, Peleg Chamberlain (Jr.) enlisted, in Aug., 1757, in Capt. Samuel Dunham's Company of Sharon (adjoining Kent), on alarm to relieve Fort William Henry. His future brother-in-law, Heman Swift, was a corporal in the same company, and one of the lieutenants of the company (Samuel Hubbell) was of Kent. The company was in service fifteen days. In the Revolutionary War. Peleg served as sergeant in Capt. Abraham Fuller's Company, 13th Regiment Connecticut Militia, which was in the City of New York in 1776. He afterwards became a resident of New Milford. By his will, which is dated June 7, 1808, and was admitted to probate at New Milford, he describes himself as of New Milford, and devises and bequeaths to his wife, Jane Chamberlain, the barn standing on her own land, one-third part of all the land of which he is possessed in his own right, all his household furniture, excepting one bed and bedding which he brought into the family, and one-half of the residue of his personal estate. To his daughter Abigail Baldwin, wife of Nathan Gaylord Baldwin, he makes a bequest, constitutes his daughter Rockselena Chamberlain his residuary legatee and devisee, and appoints his wife Jane Chamberlain and his son Swift Chamberlain executors.

Peleg Chamberlain was married twice, as follows: First, at Kent, Oct. 4, 1759, to Abigail Swift, born Dec. 1, 1740; the date of her death has not been traced. She was a daughter of Jabez Swift and his wife Abigail Pope, and a sister of Colonel and Brevet Brig.-Gen. Heman Swift, the distinguished Connecticut soldier of the Revolutionary War. Her father was a direct descendant of William Swift, who was of Watertown in 1636, and afterwards of Sandwich, where he died in 1642. His wife Joan had administration on his estate March 7, 1642-43, and survived him until 1662. The line of descent from William and Joan is: William, married Ruth, died at Sandwich, 1705; Jireh, born at Sandwich, 1665, married Abigail Gibbs, Nov. 26, 1697, died at Wareham, 1749; Jabez (father of Abigail), born at Sandwich, March 16, 1699, died at Wareham, Nov. 2, 1767, married Oct. 9, 1729, Abigail Pope, who died in 1776. Besides Abigail, Peleg Chamberlain's wife, the children of Jabez Swift and Abigail Pope were: Elisha, General Heman (died 1814), Captain Jireh, Reverend Job, Hannah, Bathsheba, Reverend Seth, and Patience (died young). Among the names of the original proprietors of Kent were those of Jabez and Zilpharet Swift and others of the same surname. Peleg Chamberlain married, second, at New Milford, date uncertain, probably about 1788, Jane Baldwin, born about 1770, daughter of Israel Baldwin of New Milford. She survived her husband, and was co-executrix, with her husband's son Swift, of his will.

Peleg Chamberlain's children as far as traced, were as follows: Abigail, named in her father's will, married Nathan Gaylord Baldwin, and died at Monkton, Vt., May 30, 1820. Her children were Electa, Isaac, Roderick, and Emmeline. Jireh, born at Kent, Nov. 29, 1762, was living in 1832; Swift, of whom below; Leander, in May, 1819, was aged 53, and was born therefore in 1765 or 1766; Rockselena, named in her father's will. Capt. Hiram Sanborn Chamberlain living (1907) at Chattanooga, Tenn. [concerning whom a biographical sketch was included in the *Annual Report of the Chamberlain Association* for 1904–5] is Leander's grandson. Jireh, Swift, and Leander, and their sister Abigail Baldwin and her husband, were pioneer settlers at Monkton, Vt., soon after the admission of Vermont into the Union. The three brothers were qualified voters there in 1798. Jireh was a selectman in 1808, and in 1812 was "of Ferrisburg," the adjoining township. Leander owned land in Ferrisburg in 1804. They were all Revolutionary War Pensioners. Jirch served in the Connecticut Militia; Swift's service is given below; and Leander served in Capt. Ephraim Kimberley's Company, 2d Connecticut Line, the same regiment that Swift served in.

AUTHORITIES

Colchester Town and Church Records.
Kent Town and Church Records.
Collections Connecticut Historical Society, vol. 9, p. 206.
Connecticut Men in the Revolution, p. 466 and pp. 365, 370, 629.
New Milford Probate, vol. 2, p. 108.
Swift Genealogy (pamphlet).
Atwater's *History of Kent.*
Heitman's *Historical Register of the Officers of the Continental Army.*
Baldwin Genealogy, pp. 120, 506.
Register of the Military Order Loyal Legion, U. S., 1906.
U. S. Pension Records.
Monkton Town Records.
Senate Documents—List of Pensioners, under the Act of March 18, 1818, printed, Washington, 1835.
Smith's *History of Addison County, Vt.,* chap. 26.
Plymouth Colony Records, Court Orders, p. 53.

SWIFT CHAMBERLAIN, 1764-1828

SWIFT CHAMBERLAIN, son of Peleg Chamberlain and his wife Abigail Swift, was born at Kent, Conn. In April, 1818, he was aged 53, and the year of his birth was therefore 1764 or 1765. He died at Monkton, Vt., Nov. 25, 1828, his gravestone says (incorrectly) in his 61st year. He was named in his father's will as co-executor with his stepmother Jane Chamberlain. In the Revolutionary War, at the age of seventeen, Swift Chamberlain, of Kent, enlisted Feb. 3, 1781, for three years, as a private in the 2d Regiment Connecticut Line, and served in that regiment continuously until its final muster out in Dec., 1783. He was in the companies of Capts. Stephen Billings, Timothy Taylor, and Aaron Benjamin, and was sergeant under the latter officer. He originally joined the 2d Connecticut in its "second formation," and, on the disbandment of the Army in June, 1783, remained in the regiment in its "final formation" and until it was disbanded in Dec., 1783. The 2d Regiment of the "final formation June-December, 1783," was one of seven regiments retained in the service after June, 1783, by General Washington's orders. The Colonel of the 2d Connecticut during 1781-83 was Colonel and Brevet Brig.-Gen. Heman Swift, Swift Chamberlain's maternal uncle. After the war, Swift Chamberlain seems to have been a school teacher at New Milford where his father probably then lived, and to have married there. His wife lived a number of years after the marriage and certainly until July, 1792. Before that date he must have thought of settling in Vermont, then recently admitted into the Union as a new State (admitted March 4, 1791), for before 1789 he had taken up land in Monkton, Addison County, Vt., as a settler, and had taken the freeman's oath. "Swift Chamberlain located about a mile northwest of the borough." On July 19, 1794, "Swift Chamberlain of New Milford" bought of Joseph Wastcott 50 acres in Monkton, of the right of Amos Northrop; and on Dec. 24, 1796, "Swift Chamberlain of Monkton" deeded land in Monkton to Abel Gunn. This deed was to secure Abel Gunn and Nathan Gaylord Baldwin (the husband of Swift's sister Abigail), who, in conjunction with Swift, had given bond to Eno Camp of New Milford that Sarah Chamberlain (apparently Swift's daughter) should, on reaching the age of 21 years in July, 1813, deed to Camp two pieces of land in New Milford. In 1798 Swift and his brothers, Jireh and Leander, were qualified voters at Monkton. After the death, in 1808, of Peleg, Swift's father, Daniel Ferris of Monkton confirmed to Swift Chamberlain, by deed of Nov. 27, 1809, "that land he sold to Peleg Chamberlain, Joseph Wastcott and Swift Chamberlain not surveyed," etc.; and in 1815 Swift witnessed a deed from his brother Jireh to his daughter Sarah. Under the Act of Congress of March 18, 1818, he applied, April 24, 1818, for a pension, which was allowed from that date, and he was put on the pension rolls Sept. 27, 1819.

Swift Chamberlain was married twice, as follows: First, at New Milford, date uncertain, probably about 1789, to Sarah Sherwood, said to have been an orphan. She died between July, 1792, and March, 1795. Second, at Bristol, Vt., March 8, 1795, to Mary Tuttle, born in 1779, daughter of Thomas Tuttle, then of Brandon, Vt. She became a U. S. pensioner in 1849, at the age of 70, survived her husband thirty years and died at Monkton, Vt., Jan. 20, 1858, in her 80th year.

His children were as follows: Of his first marriage: a child, died in infancy; Sarah, born at New Milford, July, 1792, married Edward Hall of Charlotte, Vt. Of his second marriage, all born at Monkton; HIRAM, of whom below; Amanda, born April 7, 1799, married William Porter and lived at Hudson, O.; Pamelia, born March 2, 1801; Homer, born March 4, 1804; Diantha, born Dec. 24 (record torn), said to have married Mr. Breck and lived in Newburg, O.; Jerusha, born Jan. 10, 1810, said to have married Mr. Jones and lived in Watertown, Ind.; Peleg, born Dec. 27, 1812, settled at Gouverneur, St. Lawrence County, N. Y., where he died Nov. 15, 1873. He married Selima, who survived him, and died in 1902 at Gouverneur. His daughter Leonora married Gen. Albert Milton Barney, U. S. Volunteers, and Colonel 142d Regiment New York Volunteers, and died soon after her marriage. General Barney died at New York, Aug. 24, 1886. Emily (record says Amelia), born Jan. 6, 1815, married Ryland Doten (or Doughton), lived with her mother at Monkton, in 1849, and was still living in 1874; Hector, born Jan. 13, 1817, lived in Missouri with his brother Hiram, died in 1842 and was buried at St. Charles, Mo.; Marcus, born Jan. 25, 1820, died at Gouverneur, N. Y.; his children George, Julia, and Emily (husband's name Burns) lived in

Lawrence, Mass., in 1874. Henry Martin, born Aug. 5, 1824, lived in Polk, Pa., in 1874, and is said to have been a Methodist minister.

Swift Chamberlain and his son Hiram each gave the name "Henry Martin" to one of his sons; the former to his last born (1824) the latter to his first born (1826).

AUTHORITIES

U. S. Pension Records, Widow file. 1555, Revolutionary War.
Peleg Chamberlain's will: New Milford Probate, vol. 6, p. 108.
Swift Chamberlain's Gravestone at Monkton, Vt.
Record of service of Connecticut Men in the War of the Revolution, pp. 326, 365, 366, 368, and 369.
Historical Register of Officers of the Continental Army.
Smith's History of Addison County, Vt., chap. 26, p. 514-5.
Monkton Records and Deeds.
List of Pensioners, printed, Washington, 1820.
Senate Documents, Pension Roll, printed, Washington, 1835.
Private Record printed in History of New Milford.
Mary Tuttle Chamberlain's gravestone at Monkton.
Monkton Birth Records.
Will of Peleg Chamberlain of Gouverneur, Surrogate's Records, Canton, N. Y.
Petition for Probate of same (1873).
Decree of Settlement (1902).
Records New York Commandery, M. O. Loyal Legion U. S.

HIRAM CHAMBERLAIN, 1797-1866

HIRAM CHAMBERLAIN, son of Swift Chamberlain and his wife Mary Tuttle, was born at Monkton, Vt., April 1, 1797, and died at Brownsville, Tex., Nov. 1, 1866. It is to be regretted that no memorials of the events of his boyhood and early youth are accessible, for that these would have proved interesting and instructive can hardly be doubted. When it is remembered that he was born in the log cabin of a hardy pioneer, the eldest child of a family of twelve, and probably grew up a stranger to the refinements, social intercourse, and educational privileges of older communities, the fact that, notwithstanding these disadvantages, and apparently through his own ability and unaided efforts he rose superior to his surroundings, and became a cultured, well educated man, bears testimony to a marked individuality of character that invites admiration, as well as to the dignified, self-respecting and, so far as practical, educated character of that generation of pioneer New Englanders.

In 1818 he made profession of religion at Rev. Dr. Gardner Spring's Presbyterian Church in the City of New York, and soon after entered Middlebury College in his native county in Vermont, from which he graduated in 1822. It was probably during his college life at Middlebury and earlier, that he "taught school" in Essex County, N. Y., on the opposite shore of Lake Champlain, at Lewis and Sharetown. Early in Nov., 1822, he entered Andover Theological Seminary as a student, graduating in 1825, after a course of about a year (probably in 1823-24), at Princeton Theological Seminary. Among Mr. Chamberlain's classmates at Andover were John Todd, afterwards pastor of the Congregational church at Pittsfield, Mass.; Jacob Abbott, author of the Rollo books and Franconia books; John Maltby, afterwards pastor Hammond St. Congregational Church at Bangor, Me. Prof. Leonard Bacon (Yale); Rev. George W. Blagden, Old South Church, Boston; Prof. George Sheppard (Bangor); and Rev. Edward Beecher (brother of Henry Ward) were all fellow students of Mr. Chamberlain at Andover, but in other classes.

It is of course impossible at this time to recover the details of his student career; but at the completion of his educational course in his 29th year, there is every indication that he was of high personal character, of great promise and able to make and keep friends whose interest must have been due to attractive qualities.

In the spring of 1825, Mr. Chamberlain took an active and prominent part in the movement which had its rise at Andover, looking to the establishment of a National Domestic Missionary Society, and with which the origin and subsequent organization (in 1826) of the American Home Missionary Society was directly and closely connected. One result of this interest in home missions was shown in the determination of six Andover graduates of 1825, Mr. Chamberlain among the number, to devote themselves to missionary labors in the Western and Southern States. To that end four of these, Messrs. Pomeroy, Alden, Ellis, and Bingham, were ordained in the Old South Church, Boston, Sept. 29, 1825; and another, Mr. Foster, at Rutland, Vt., Oct. 19, 1825. Mr. Chamberlain being a member of Dr. Spring's church in New York received ordination as an evangelist or missionary from the New York Presbytery, Oct. 16, 1825. Ten days after his ordination Mr. Chamberlain and his first wife were married at Dorset, Vt., and immediately thereafter, in furtherance of the resolution made at Andover, he removed to Missouri, where, under commission from the United Domestic Missionary Society of New York, he entered upon his career of missionary work at St. Louis, remaining in that city until 1827, in which year he beame the pastor at "Dardonne," Mo. From 1828 to 1834, he was the pastor at Boonville, Mo., being also, in 1828, agent of the Amerian Home Missionary Society. He was the pastor at New Franklin and Fayette, Mo., in 1834 and 1835, and also, in 1834, agent of Marion College. During the years from 1835 to 1841 his pastorate duties were at St. Charles, Mo., and from the latter year until early in 1845 he edited and published the *Herald of Religious Liberty* at St. Louis. Relinquishing the editorial chair of the *Herald*, he removed to Tennessee, and became the pastor at Memphis from 1845 to 1847, and at Somerville and Bethany from 1847 to 1850. In the latter year in the most southerly part of distant Texas—only then recently admitted as a State of the Union —he became the pastor at Brownsville (the Fort Brown of the Mexican War) on the lower Rio Grande, opposite Matamoros, Mexico. There he continued to reside, engaged in the work of his pastorate, until his death in 1866, having faithfully and ably devoted forty years of his life to the cause of Home Missions. No voluntary, self-denying promise was ever more sacredly kept and resolutely redeemed. The Presbyterian Church at Brownsville, the first Protestant church on the Rio Grande, was erected through his instrumentality, and stood as a fitting monument to his influence, ability, and devotion until its destruction in the tornado of 1867. At the time of his death Mr. Chamberlain was Worshipful Master of Rio Grande Lodge No. 81, F. A. M., and District Deputy Grand Master of the Grand Lodge of the State of Texas.

"And when they buried him, the little port
Had seldom seen a costlier funeral."

Hiram Chamberlain was married thrice as follows: First, at Dorset, Vt., Oct. 26, 1825, to Maria Morse; born at West Hartford, Conn. (parentage and date of birth not traced), died at New Franklin, Mo., March 24, 1835, and was buried there with an infant son.

Second, in Missouri (probably at St. Charles), April 19, 1836, to Sarah H. Wardlaw; born at New Providence, Rockbridge County, Va. (parentage and date of birth not traced), died in May, 1840, and lies buried at her place of birth.

Third, at Pinckney, Mo., Oct. 16, 1842, to Anna Adelia Griswold, born at Wethersfield, Conn., April 12, 1816, daughter of William Griswold and Aura Case, died at Brooklyn, N. Y., Nov. 24, 1882, and was buried at Brownsville, Tex. She was a direct lineal descendant of Edward Griswold, immigrant and progenitor, who came from Warwickshire, England, and settled at Windsor, Conn., in 1639; the line of ancestry being Edward, George, Benjamin, Benjamin, Sylvanus, William, Anna Adelia.

Hiram Chamberlain's children were as follows: Of his first marriage: Henry Martin, born at St. Louis, Mo., Sept. 25, 1826, died soon after birth; Henrietta Maria, born July 21, 1832, residing at Corpus Christi, Tex.; married Capt. Richard King. (Her children were Henrietta, wife of Brig.-Gen. Edward Atwood, U. S. A.; Ella, wife of Louis Welton; Richard, married Elizabeth Pearl Ashbrook; Alice, wife of Robert Kleberg; and Lee, died unmarried.) Payson Dwight, born at New Franklin, Mo., March 4, 1835, died soon after birth and was buried with his mother. Of his second marriage, there were no children. Of his third marriage: Hiram, born at St. Charles, Mo., April 28, 1843, married Mattie Wiesiger, died childless at Danville, Ky., July, 1879; Milton Griswold, born at St. Louis, Mo., Sept. 11, 1845, died June 16, 1847; Daniel Baker, born at Somerville, Tenn., Nov. 24, 1847, died young; Peter Bland, born at Somerville, Tenn., Dec. 18, 1848, died 1882, married Filipa. (His children were Albert, Bland, Carrie, Virginia, Minnie, Alice, Adelina.) William Chapman, born at Brownsville, Tex., Oct. 2, 1850, residing at Laredo, Tex., is married and has several children; James Wardlaw, born at Brownsville, Tex., 1852, died young; ADELIA, wife of Col. William J. Harding of Brooklyn, N. Y.; Edwin, born at Brownsville, Tex., Nov. 30, 1857, residing at San Antonio, Tex.; married Adelaide Gillette, daughter of Fidelio B.

and Sarah Gillette, a direct lineal descendant of William Gillette, a Huguenot refugee from Rochelle, France, who settled in Connecticut about 1688—the line being William, Elisha, Fidelio Buckingham, Abram Dunn, Fidelio Buckingham, Adelaide. (His surviving children are Fidelio Gillette, a graduate of Princeton University, class of '07, and Edmund.)

AUTHORITIES

Middlebury College Records and General Catalogue.
Andover Theological Seminary Records and General Catalogue.
Princeton Theological Seminary Records and General Catalogue.
Family Archives.
Thompson's *Vermont* (year 1842).
History of the Origin and Organization of the American Home Missionary Society by Rev. Nathaniel Bouton, D. D., of Concord, N. H., New York, 1860.
Herald of Religious Liberty, vol. 1, No. 28, St. Louis, December 26, 1844, No. 31, January 16, 1845.
Monkton, Vermont, Records.
Gravestones of Hiram and Anna A. Chamberlain at Brownsville, Tex.
Griswold Family Genealogical Record in possession of Col. Wm. J. Harding.
Memoir of A. D. Gillette, New York, Ward & Drummond, 1883.

JOHN CHAMBERLAIN, THE QUAKER

By Eben Putnam

The persecution of John Chamberlain [son of Henry Chamberlain of Hingham, England, and of Hingham, New England], for his Quaker belief, is a striking illustration of the manner in which the government of the Massachusetts Bay attempted to regulate not only religious but civil matters.

The actions and teachings of the earlier adherents of Fox, in England, had caused dismay. The orderly and tolerant way of living, later the distinctive mark of the Society of Friends, was by no means characteristic of the early disciples of Fox. It was even feared that the self-appointed messengers to New England were really emissaries of Rome. The authorities of Massachusetts Bay, holding that their charter gave them the right to exclude undesirable inhabitants, did not hesitate to attempt to prevent the residence within the limits of their charter of any person to whose way of life they objected. The Quaker propaganda was distinctly contrary to and disagreeable to Puritan ideas, and the persistence of those who, by both reasonable and sensational methods, sought to force upon the people consideration of their claims, was not only provoking and tantalizing to a degree we cannot realize, but was deemed dangerous to the existing order of things—as indeed it was. The grave mistake of the authorities was in taking notice of the fanatics, for such were the new comers. This precipitated the trouble, and the evident injustice meted out to those who harbored and gave hearing to Quaker enthusiasts, caused a wave of sympathy to spread through the country, and secured for the sect many adherents. John Chamberlain was a currier. He had married, May 19, 1653, Ann, daughter of William Brown, and had at least four children born prior to 1660. An account of his conversion to Quaker doctrine is of record. He attended, Oct. 27, 1659, the execution of William Robinson and Marmaduke Stevenson on Boston Common, seeing there also, the reprieve of Mary Dyer after the halter had been placed about her neck. They suffered death, not because of their religious belief, but because they had deliberately broken the law in remaining after banishment, evidently with the intention of suffering the death penalty, as a few months before they had been released from prison and ordered to leave the jurisdiction of Massachusetts upon pain of death. John Chamberlain states he was present at their execution, and was drawn to visit those in prison, "and soon tasted of your cruelty, and hath been much and long imprisoned by you; and, although still you have sorely shot at him, yet his bow abides in strength, being enabled to bear all your cruelty, and stand as a faithful witness for the Lord against you."

At a Court of Assistants held March 5-13, 1659-60, four months after this, he was among a party of nine, some from Salem, where they had been arrested, others from Boston, and one, Martha Stanly "late of Tenterdon in Kent, single woman," who "had a message from the Lord to visit her friends in prison in Boston," who were examined regarding their doctrine. Of Chamberlain the clerk's record reads, "John Chamberlain of Boston came into Court with his Hatt on." Moreover, he expressed himself "yt [that] he find not [the] ye opinion of ye Quakers to be cursed but yt which shall stand when all yors [yours] shall fall."

The other evidence apparently was not of a character far different from Chamberlain's, except in the case of the Salem contingent and the Kentish woman. Mary Trask, Margaret Smith, and Martha Stanly could not be kept from expressing their opinions, and had to be removed from Court. Concerning the claims of the Quakers for recognition, it was related that "Major Hawthorne at Dinner with ye Governor and magistrates at a Court of Assistants said that at Salem Cassandra Southwick said she was greater than Moses because Moses had seen God but twice and that backwards, but she had seen him three times face to face, named place, viz., her old House one time and by such a swamp another time," etc.

The record proceeds: "the jury was called over to them and liberty given to challenge any of them off the Bench."

No record appears of sentence or commitment at this court, but May 25 following a writ of arrest was issued against Chamberlain as follows:

"To ye keeper of ye Prison at Boston

"You are to take into your custody ye person of John Chamberline for venting his wretched opinions in Charlestowne meetinge howse tendinge to seduce and for reproachfull expressions otherwise. You are to keepe him as a prisoner untill Authoryty heere established take farther coorce with him: Charlestowne ye 25: 3: 1660

"Per me RICHARD RUSSELL."

The General Court, perceiving that their measures had been too harsh and that some concession must be made to the rising popular indignation, had passed a law, May 22, 1661, which permitted a "vagabond" Quaker to return to try the patience of the authorities no less than six times before the death penalty was exacted. Quakers arising from the people themselves, those who had right of residence in the country, were liable to the law of 1658, and were to be banished under penalty of death if they returned. On May 22, 1661, after passing the law mentioned, the court granted Winlock Christison, who was among those examined in March, 1660, and others, liberty to leave its jurisdiction, but ordering them to be conveyed from town to town on their way by the constable. Two of the prisoners, because of standing mute at their trial, were to be tied to the cart's tail, and receive twenty lashes in Boston. Christison had been sentenced to die, June 13, but on June 6 he was given liberty to ask for mercy, and on June 11 was escorted beyond the limits of Dedham by the Constable, whose return is on file.

We have now come to the interesting and valuable petition of Henry Chamberlain, Sr., and Jr., which was evidently presented at this time, and we may suspect with the hope that he would eventually abandon his opinions.

"To the Honorable Generall Court now assembled at Boston the Humble petition of Henry Chamberlayne senior and Henry Chamberlayne junior Humbly sheweth

"That forasmuch one John Chamberlayne a very neere & deare Naturall relation of ors a child a brother doth now ly shutt up unto death there beinge no thinge between him & the uttmost execution of humane Justice but the pronunciation of Judgment we having bin & still remayninge petitioners unto God for mercy in his behalfe, we know not unto whom to Cry next but unto yourselves Naturall affection is alwayes urginge of us to doe somethinge in order to the further contynuation of his life & what to doe we know not loath we are to offend God or you loath we are to obstruct Justice & yet fayne wee woulde plead for mercy, & we have some hopes that the Honr Court may at least moderate Justice by mercy as to cause them to goe together as to this particular Administration.

"Or Humble petition therefore to this Honred Court is that if it may stand with the Justice of God's glory & the preservation of our Just lawes agaynst Quakers you would be pleased to remitt the sentence of Banishment upon Payne of Death, & permitt him to live in prison dureing your pleasure, we still hopeing yt God may enlarge his soule from those Chaynes of Darknes & then & not till then, we should be bold to petition for the enlargement of his body from outward restraynt, wee should not have bin so bould to have mentioned such a thinge to this Honed Court, but that we thought his condition somewhat more capable of mercy then the condition of other Quakers, he being an Inhabitant a child to a father a father to children, & so bound by many obligations of naturall relation unto this place, we hope he may have accomodation in prison to worke at his Trade for the support of himself & his which if this Honed Court be pleased to graunt it will abundantly engage your poore petitioners to pray etc.

"In answer to this pet the deputyes thinke meet to order that John Chamberlayne now in prison be forthwith removed to the Castle Iland there to provide himself lodging housinge victualls etc. at his owne charge & dureinge the Courts pleasure to remayne there & not to Come off at his perill desireing our Honed magistrates consent hereto.

7 : 4 : 1661   "WILLIAM TORREY CLERIC."

According to Bishop, Chamberlain had been whipped nine times by Sept. 9, 1661. He had added to his "crime" by marrying with Catharine Chatham, who "came from London through many travels and hard trials to Boston and appeared clothed with sackcloth as a sign of the indignation of the Lord coming upon you." She had been imprisoned and whipped.

In Nov., 1661, the letter of the King directing that the laws in force against the Quakers be repealed, was received, and the General Court took occasion to place on record that all the prisoners had been granted liberty to leave and had done so. Evidently Chamberlain had received his liberty and had removed with his family to Newport, where he was in Aug., 1664, the date of birth of his daughter Susanna. According to the Quaker records he died April, 1666, but the same records note the birth of his youngest child, Jane, in Dec., 1667. His children were Ann, John, Elizabeth, Henry, William (who removed to Shrewsbury, N. J.), Susanna, Peleg, and Jane.

AUTHORITIES

Massachusetts Archives, vol. 10, 266 et seq.
Records of Massachusetts, 1650-1664.
Bishop's *New England Judged*.
Austin's *Genealogical Dictionary of Rhode Island*.

HUGH CHAMBERLEN, JR.

HUGH CHAMBERLEN, M. D., 1664-1728

Hugh Chamberlen, Jr., was the eldest son of Hugh Chamberlen, Sr., and was descended from William Chamberlen, a Huguenot, who migrated in 1569 to Southampton, England, from Paris. He was born in 1664, and was educated at Trinity College, Cambridge, of which house he was a Fellow Commoner. He received the degree of A.M., in 1683 *per literas regias*. On Oct. 30, 1684, Hugh Chamberlen, Jr., settled at Leyden, and entered on the Physic line. On Oct. 8, 1689, he was created Doctor of Medicine at Cambridge (*Comitiis Regiis*).

The following excerpts from the "Annals of the College of Physicians" show his connection with that body:

Jan. 6, 1693, Dr. Hugh Chamberlen of Trinity College in Cambridge, who was created Doctor of Physick at Cambridge, Oct. 8, 1689, as appeared by his diploma, was examined the first time in Physiologia in order to be admitted a Candidate and was approved.

Feb. 3, 1693, Dr. Chamberlen was a second time examined and approved.

March 3, 1693, Dr. Chamberlen was a third time examined in Therapeuticks and was approved but with this admonition that he should more diligently apply himselfe to the therapeutick part of physick.

Postri die Festi Palmarum 1693. Dr. Hugh Chamberlen was proposed and admitted Candidate. He gave his faith to his observation of the statutes and subscribed them.

Nov. 3, 1693, Dr. Chamberlen complained of one Cort, a surgeon, for bleeding and prescribeing internall medicins for Mrs. Hermitage in the Collick and rheumatism without the advice of Dr. Chamberlen who was her physician, the said Cort declaring there was no need of any physician although Dr. Chamberlen had been concerned there before and whom they were necessitated to send for again.

Dec. 1, 1693, Dr. Chamberlen Complained of one Cort, a surgeon who had not onely prescribed internall medicins and bled Mrs. Hermitage his patient but had also spoke slightingly and scandalously of him all which Cort denied though Dr. Chamberlen brought the bill from the Apothecaryes to whom he had prescribed the medicins. The President forbidd Cort to practise and ordered the Beadle to take care of him about it.

April 2, 1694, Dr. Hugh Chamberlen was proposed balloted and admitted a Fellow. He gave his faith to observe the Statutes.

Sept. 30, 1707, Hugh Chamberlen, Junior, was proposed, balloted, elected, and sworn a Censor, to which honourable position he was again chosen on Sept. 30, 1719, and again on Nov. 10, 1721. Feb. 14, 1722-23, he resigned the office because of ill health.

The life of Hugh Chamberlen, Jr., was, compared with that of his father and grandfather, calm and uneventful. He was no enthusiast, either in religion or politics, nor was he full of projects for his own or other people's welfare. Materials for compiling a biography of him are consequently scarce. A few scraps, however, have been collected and are here given.

Swift, in his *Journal* to Stella, writes Nov. 5, 1710:—"I was with Mr. Harley from dinner to seven this night, and went to the Coffee-house where Dr. D'Avenant would fain have had me gone and drink a bottle of wine at his house hard by, with

Dr. Chamberlen; but the puppy used so many words, that I was afraid of his company; and though we promised to come at eight, I sent a messenger to him, that Chamberlen was going to a patient, and therefore we would put it off till another time; so he, and the Comptroller and I, were prevailed on by Sir Matthew Dudley to go to his house, where I stayed till twelve, and left them."

From the printed catalogues of the Fellows of the College of Physicians it is found that Hugh Chamberlen, Jr., left his house in Essex Street in 1717, and went to live in King Street, Covent Garden, then the most fashionable part of London. He had at this time succeeded in establishing himself not only as a popular obstetrician, but as a trustworthy physician, and he practiced as both among the higher classes of society.

Hugh Chamberlen, Jr., was a friend of Atterbury, Bishop of Rochester, and in 1723 he was permitted by warrant to visit the Bishop, who was confined in the Tower, in the place of Dr. Freind, when this physician also became a prisoner in the Tower. Dr. Freind mentions Hugh Chamberlen in his work on smallpox, published in 1719, and in his fifth *History* styles him, "Peritissimus H. Chamberlen."

Hugh Chamberlen, Jr., was married three times, and had three daughters—Mary, by his first wife, Anna Maria and Charlott by his second. His third wife, Lady Crew, who was the daughter of Sir Willoughby Aston, Bart., and relict of Sir Thomas Crew, of Utkington in Cheshire, Kt., survived him, and died suddenly April 6, 1734. His first wife was Mary, only daughter and heiress of Nathaniel Bacon, Esq., of Friston, and by this marriage he became possessed of the Manors of Alderton Hall. His daughter Mary died unmarried. Anna Maria married that distinguished statesman, the Rt. Hon. Edward Hopkins, M. P. for Coventry in the time of King William III and Queen Anne, and Secretary of State for Ireland. She died Feb. 9, 1768, aged 67, and was buried at Coventry. Charlott married Richard Luther, Esq., of Myles, in Essex, and this estate continued for many years the undivided property in equal moieties of their descendants.

[These extracts from *The Chamberlens*, by J. H. Aveling, M.D., F.S.A., and the plates for the portrait and the cenotaph, were sent by Dr. J. W. Chamberlin for use in this Report. The father of the first wife of Hugh Chamberlen, Jr., was Nathaniel Bacon, of Bacon's Rebellion in Virginia, son of Thomas Bacon of Friston Hall.]

CENOTAPH IN WESTMINSTER ABBEY

MONUMENT IN WESTMINSTER ABBEY

Epitaph by Bishop Atterbury

Translation from the Latin by Dr. J. W. Browne

Hugh Chamberlen
of Hugh and Peter, both physicians,
The Son and Grandson,
Like these, followed Medicine successfully and singularly adorned his Calling:
Who to the utmost skill in his Art
So joined perfect Honesty of Word and Deed,
Extraordinary Purity of Mind
And Gentleness of Manners,
That whether to the Whole or to the Sick he came more welcome,
Whether he were better Man or Physician,
Has been eagerly disputed among those
Who with one voice agree to proclaim Him
In both characters Foremost.
Skilled in not one but every branch of Healing
To the perils of childbearing in women,
And to the diseases of Infants
He gave his most anxious pains:
And herein oftenest was it His care
That noble families were not bereft of their only Heirs
And his beloved Country of eminent Citizens.
All alike he had the Will not less than the Power to serve,
And thereto, when the State was rent by Faction,
He piously extended even to those whose opinions were not his
His Friendship and to them too freely imparted the resources of his Skill.
The Elegance and Splendour of his Life,
The Strength and Loftiness of his Mind
The inbred Generosity of his bent,
The Frankness and Nobility of his very Bearing,
Had been sure proofs to all
That his stock was of no ignoble Origin:
Even tho' they knew not that he traced his descent thro' 400 years
To the Illustrious race of the Ancient Earls of Tankerville.

Familiar with every Rank and Condition of Life,
He claimed and received from all his due and Honour,

An intimate of the Great he preserved his self-respect.
Of the Meanest, his Courtesy and kindness.
His zeal of well-doing admitting of no distinction.
To both alike he became at once Benefactor and Friend.
A Son, he was of wonderful duty and affection toward his Father.
A Father of his daughters most loving;
Of Them he had three, one by his first, two by his second wife,
Chaste and Good, most like to their Mothers.
With all of these to the day of his death he lived in closest bonds of love,
His third Wife he left to survive him.
To these social and Domestic Virtues
There failed not the Crown of
A deep sense and love of Religion
And an awful reverence for its Great Source:
Upborne by these his Soul,
Now ripe to burst through the slough of this body,
Nor drawing feebleness from the languors of a long disease.
Aspired to Heaven,
And, finally closing this Life of Mortality.
(Yet a life not wasted but full of good fruits)
With a death most truly Christian,
Soared to its Heavenly Home.
He died on the 17th day of June In the Year of our
Lord 1728, and in the 64th year of his life
Worthy indeed to have lived a longer life,
To whose skill only it was due that many
Were not early snatched away midst their first wailings,
But even now survive to the utmost limits of old age.

To This Man Most Upright, most dear,
For Life saved at birth,
For Health so often restored
And at length assured,
Edmund Duke of Buckingham
Has raised this monument and Tomb,
Ennobled by His Effigy,
And with statues set on either side
(Fashioned upon the model of an ancient marble),
To the end that they may bear witness to posterity
How great has been the Debt due to Him,
This Acknowledgment how poor.

This epitaph was engraved upon a magnificent cenotaph erected, doubtless at the suggestion of his mother, by the youthful Edmund, Duke of Buckingham. Dean Stanley tells us in his *History of Westminster Abbey*, that by a Chapter order of May 16, 1729 (afterwards rescinded) the Duchess of Buckingham was "allowed to take down the screen of the sacrarium to erect the monument." It was eventually placed in the north aisle of the choir, and is thus described by Neale:—

"The monument of Hugh Chamberlen, M. D., which is the first that engages attention on the south side, is a very handsome composition of white and variegated marbles. It principally consists of an inscribed basement, a sarcophagus, several figures, a pyramid, and a circular pediment (with mantling) rising from pilasters of the Doric Order. On the sarcophagus is a finely executed statue of the deceased, in his Doctor's gown, reclining upon a mattress; his right arm being supported by cushions, and his hand extended on his cap; in his left hand he holds a book, which also rests upon his knee. There is much ease and gracefulness in the position of this figure; the features are expressive and penetrating, and the drapery well cast. At the sides of the sarcophagus, on receding pedestals, are statues of Health and Longevity; the cup and serpent which distinguished the former are now broken; the latter is resting her right hand upon a shield, on which are sculptured a lion couchant and a soaring eagle. On the pyramid is a winged boy, or angel, bearing a wreath and a trumpet, and two other boys are seated on the ascending sides of the pediment, each upholding a medallion of a female. The sculptors were Peter Schumakers and Laur Delvaux." Arms: painted. Sab, an Escutcheon Arg., within an Orle of Cinquefoils, Or, Chamberlen.

In the British Museum is to be found, "The Catalogue of the Library of Hugh Chamberlen, M. D., lately deceased to be sold very cheap on Tuesday April 2nd, 1734, beginning at eight in the morning by Fletcher Gyles bookseller over against Gray's Inn in Holborn." It contained 1734 volumes, 165 of which were medical books.

A CHAMBERLAINE FAMILY OF GLOUCESTERSHIRE, ENGLAND

Compiled by Jenny Chamberlain Watts

It was the duty of the Heralds' College, in England, to supervise the bearing of arms by the gentry, permitting none unless duly authorized. To accomplish this, two of the three kings-at-arms,—Norroy in charge of the region north of the Trent, and Clarenceux south of the Trent,—visited personally or by deputy at given intervals every county town in their respective divisions, and summoned the gentry of the neighborhood to appear, and prove title to their armorial bearings, and record the pedigrees of their families, in order that the Heralds' College might so far as possible have complete and accurate lists of all the people in the kingdom entitled to bear arms. During the visitation of Gloucestershire in 1683 there was recorded the pedigree of "Chamberlaine of Maugersbury in Stow." The lesser officials of the Heralds' College were six heralds (Windsor, Chester, Lancaster, Richmond, Somerset, York) and four pursuivants (Rouge Croix, Blue Mantle, Rouge Dragon, Portcullis). Hence this pedigree appears in a manuscript in the Heralds' College entitled, *The Visitation of the County of Gloucester, begun by Thomas May, Chester, and Gregory King, Rouge Dragon, in Trinity Vacation, 1682, and finished by Henry Dethick, Richmond, and the said Rouge Dragon, Pursuivant, in Trinity Vacation, 1683, by virtue of several Deputations from Sir Henry St. George, Kt., Clarenceux King of Arms.* This was printed by T. Fitz-Roy Fenwick, M.A., and Walter C. Metcalfe, F.S.A., at Exeter, England, in 1884, from the original manuscript preserved in the Heralds' College. The text given below follows this copy verbatim, simply translating into words the signs for marriage, descent, and the like, of its tabular arrangement. In 1866 Sir Thomas Phillipps, Bart., printed a part of this *Visitation* of 1683, adding considerable material. His additions to the Chamberlaine pedigree, so far as they concern the earlier generations, are printed below in *italics*. The additions made by the editor of this Report are enclosed in brackets. The two books quoted most frequently are: *The Ancient and Present State of Gloucestershire*, by Sir Robert Atkyns, Knight (1646–1711), a landowner and resident in Gloucestershire (2d ed., 1768); and *Historical, Monumental, and Genealogical Collections relative to the County of Gloucester, printed from the original papers of the late Ralph Bigland, Esq., Garter Principal King of Arms*, two volumes, 1786–1792. Both works are rare folios.

It is hoped that some reader of this pedigree will furnish information regarding the American immigrant mentioned,—Thomas Chamberlaine of Virginia, who married Mary, daughter of Abraham Wood of Virginia. The following extracts from the *Virginia Magazine of History and Biography* locate him in Henrico County:—

"A deed was recorded in Henrico in December, 1686, from Thos. Chamberlayne and Mary his wife, daughter of Major-General Abraham Wood, conveying to George Archer and Joseph Royall, land which had been devised to them by General Wood." (Vol. 8, p. 76.)

"Major-General Abraham Wood, who resided near the present site of Petersburg, was long a prominent and influential man. He was a Burgess for Henrico [October, 1644]; February, 1644–45; November, 1645; March, 1645–46; October, 1646 (when he was entitled captain). At the session of October, 1646, it was enacted that Captain Abraham Wood, 'whose service hath been employed at Fort Henry' (on the Appomattox), should be granted the fort and six hundred acres adjoining on the condition that he kept ten armed men there for three years. In November, 1652, as Major Abraham Wood, he was Burgess for Charles City; and again in November, 1654. In December, 1656, as Lieutenant-Colonel Abraham Wood, he was again a member of the House, and at the same session was appointed colonel of the regiment of Charles City and Henrico, in the place of Edward Hill. In March, 1657–58, he was elected a member of the Council, and continued for a number of years to form one of that body. One of his daughters is said to have married Peter Jones, one of the family from whom Petersburg derived its name; and another, as the Henrico records show, married Major Thomas Chamberlayne of that county." (Vol. 3, p. 252, note.)

According to Mr. William G. Stanard, Librarian of the Virginia Historical Society, Thomas Chamberlaine was a member of the House of Burgesses for Charles City County in 1695.

CHAMBERLAINE OF MAUGERSBURY IN STOW

Arms.—Quarterly of 6. 1 and 6, *Gules an inescutcheon Argent, within an orle of mullets Or;* 2, *Gules a chevron between three escallops Or;* 3, *Azure five lions rampant 3 and 2 Or (Gatesden);* 4, *Ermine a chief indented Gules (Mortein);* 5, *Azure two lions passant gardant Or and a label of three points Argent (Ekney).*

1 SIR THOMAS[1] CHAMBERLAINE of Prestbury, co. Glouc. Ambassador to Hen. 8, Edw. 6, and Queen Elizabeth, died the latter end of Queen Elizabeth. 1st wife: Lady Anne Vander Zenny, a Low Dutch Woman [of the House of Nassau], s. p. 2d. wife: Elizabeth, dau. of Sr John Ludington of the North and widow of ———— Machin. 3. wife: [Anne, daughter of Kirkeet. Prestbury lies seven miles northeast of the city of Gloucester. Before the Reformation it belonged to the bishops of Hereford, who "erected in this parish a handsome stone house, which was moated round." After the dissolution of the religious foundations, "Sir Thomas Chamberlain . . . obtained a long lease of this manor, and resided in this place. . . . Reginald Nicholas, a servant to sir John Chamberlain," son of Sir Thomas, "purchased a grant of the rever-

sion of the manor, and supplanted his master" as lord of the manor before 1608. (Atkyns.) In 1552 (6 Ed. VI) the manors of Oddington, Church Down, Hucclecot, Compton-Abdale, Bishop's Norton, Shurdington magna, Uphatherley (Hatherley Upper), and Witcomb, which had all in former days belonged to the Archbishop of York, were granted to "Sir Thomas Chamberlayne, otherwise Tankerville, Knight." (Atkyns and Bigland.) Sir Thomas Chamberlayne, Chief-Justice of Chester in 1616 (died 1625), was his nephew, the son of his brother William. (*Dict. of Nat. Biog.*)]

Sons by second wife:
i SIR JOHN[2] CHAMBERLAINE of Prestbury, m. Elizabeth, dau. of [Sir Thomas?] Thinne of Longleat, co. Wilts, ob. s. p. [He was lord of the manors of Church Down, Hucclecot, Shurdington magna, Uphatherley, and Witcomb in 1608. In 1612 "Sir John Chamberlaine mortgaged the Manor Mansion, and Estate of Witcomb to Dame Elizabeth Hickes, widow of Sir Michael Hickes, Secretary to Lord Burleigh, for securing £2,200." She foreclosed, and in 1616 received from Sir John and his trustees an absolute title (Bigland)].
2 ii EDMUND[2] CHAMBERLAINE of Maugersbury.
Daughter by second wife:
THEOPHILA,[2] mar. ———— Hughes, M.D.
Son by third wife:
3 [THOMAS[2]] CHAMBERLAINE of Oddington (b. about 1568).

2 EDMUND[2] CHAMBERLAINE [*Thomas*[1]] of Maugersbury, co. Glouc. ob. circa 1634. 1st wife: Anne, dau. of ——————— and widow of Moulton of Surrey, s. p. 2d wife: Grace, dau. of [John] Strangeways of Melbury, co. Dorset. [He purchased the manors of Stow and Maugersbury in 1603, and indulged in a long litigation with "the Stow people as to market dues and other manerial perquisites in which the latter lost their cause and were mulcted heavily in costs." (Bigland.) These manors lie eighteen miles northeast of the city of Gloucester. "He was high-sheriff of Glocestershire 39 Eliz." (Atkyns.) In 1608 he had ten men servants "fit for His Majesty's service in the Wars." He died April 12, 1634. His wife Grace survived him. He was possessed of the manor of Stow, *alias* Stow on the Old (Wold), *alias* Stow St. Edward, and the manor of Malgersbury, *alias* Mawgersbury, both of which he held of the King in chief by knight's service, each by the twentieth part of a knight's fee. Three "messuages and 6½ virgates of land,"—that is, three homesteads and about 200 acres,—belonging to the manor of Maugersbury, were settled upon the second son, Edmund,[3] for the term of eighty years. Of the manors of Stow and Maugersbury, one-third was settled upon the eldest son John[3] and his wife Elizabeth, and two-thirds were settled upon the widow Grace for life with reversion to the son John.[3] This was by indenture dated Oct. 12, 1631, executed in anticipation of John's marriage. Edmund[2] was, also, at his death, "seised in fee-tail of one capital messuage in Presbury with a garden, orchard, yard, etc., thereto belonging," which he "held of the King as of his manor of East Greenwich . . . in free and common socage and not . . . by knight's service"; also a reversion of "one

house or tenement in Stowe and the lands thereto belonging lying in the common fields of Netherswell and Overwell," and "one close in Stow called Gill Stevens," in both of which Joan Freeman held a life interest. These lands were held of the King by the same tenure as the house in Prestbury. (*Abstracts of Gloucestershire Inquisitiones post mortem*, 1625-36, ed. by W. P. W. Phillimore and George S. Fry, pp. 208-211. British Record Society, Index Library, vol. 9.) Presumably this did not represent all of his estate, as lands owned by his father, Sir Thomas, and his elder brother, Sir John, of whom he was the heir, are found later in the possession of his great-grandson,—for instance the manors of Church Down and Shurdington. A view of the manor-house of Maugersbury (about 1700), and the coat of arms of the family, appear at p. 365 of Atkyns.]

Daughter by second wife:
 GRACE,[3] wife of Edmund Webb of Rodburne Cheney, Wilts, after to Thomas Whyte of Even Swyndon, Wilts.
Sons by second wife:
4 i JOHN[3] CHAMBERLAINE of Maugersbury, Esq. [b. about 1609.]
5 ii EDMUND,[3] [b. about 1611.]

3 [THOMAS[2] CHAMBERLAYNE (*Thomas*[1]) of Oddington, two miles east of Stow. In 1608 he was "a subsidy man," was lord of this manor, and had four servants "fit for His Majesty's service in the Wars." His tombstone, in the chancel of the church at Oddington, reads: " Here lyeth the body of Thomas Chamberlayne, Esqr., descended from ye Earles of Tancrevile, High Chamberlaynes of Normandy. He was third son of Sir Thomas Chamberlayne of Prestbury, in the County of Glouc. Knight, Ambassadour from Hen. 8, Edw. 6, Q. Mary, and Q. Elizabeth, to ye Q. of Hungary, to ye K. of Sweden, and to ye K. of Portugal, and to Phillip ye 2d King of Spaine. He marryed Margaret, daughter and heyre of Edward Bagehott, of Prestbury aforesaid, Gent., who also lies interred here. By her he left five sons, Thomas, John, Leonard, George, and Edward, and 5 daughters Ann, Margaret, Mary, Frances, and Elizabeth. He dyed ye 4th of Decr. 1640, aged 72. This Monument was erected at ye cost and charges of John Chamberlane, M. Art. and Med. Proyfessor." (Bigland.)

Sons:
 i THOMAS,[3] b. Dec., 1599. His tombstone in the chancel at Oddington reads: "Here lyeth the body of Thomas Chamberlayne, Esqr., born in December, 1599, died the 17 of May, 1689, eldest son of Thomas Chamberlayne, buried hereby. Here lyeth the body of Katherine only daughter of Robert Brent, Esqr., and only wife of Thomas Chamberlayne, here near interred. She was born 1610, married 1630, and died 26 Oct., 1683." (Bigland.) His will, made in 1687, mentions two sons, *Thomas* and *Robert*, as then living; the daughter of his son *John*, deceased, and two children of his son *Thomas*; also six daughters. An abstract of his will is given below among the *Abstracts from the Prerogative Court of Canterbury*, which follow this pedigree.
 ii JOHN.[3]
 iii LEONARD.[3]
 iv GEORGE.[3]

v EDWARD,[3] b. at Oddington, Dec. 13, 1616; d. at Chelsea, near London, May, 1703. He entered St. Edmund Hall, Oxford, at Michaelmas, 1634; received the degree of B.A. April 20, 1638; M.A. March 6, 1641; LL.D., at Cambridge, Jan., 1670-71; D.C.L., at Oxford, 1672. "He was one of the original members of the Royal Society." Among other books, he was the author of *Anglia Notitia, or the Present State of England*. This handbook, first published in 1669, passed through twenty editions during his lifetime. He m. in 1658 Susannah, daughter of Richard Clifford, and had nine children. She d. Dec. 17, 1703. John[4] (1666-1723), son of Edward,[3] continued his father's literary work. "According to contemporary report, he knew sixteen languages." He was a fellow of the Royal Society in 1702, and was the author of many books. Biographies of both father and son appear in the *Dictionary of National Biography*, edited by Leslie Stephen. Atkyns (p. 508) wrote about 1700: "Thomas Chamberlain, esq., is the present lord of the manor [of Oddington], who has a seat here, and an estate in this and other places, . . . John Chamberlayn, of Westminster, esq., is the heir male of this branch of the family; he is likewise the heir, by his mother, of the ancient family of the Cliffords of Frampton upon Severn, in this county; he is the author of that most useful publick book, 'The Present State of England'; and has many ways distinguished himself by his great application to the publick service of his country."]

4 JOHN[3] CHAMBERLAINE [*Thomas,[1] Edmund[2]*] of Maugersbury, Esq., ob. 1668, æt. 59, mar. at *Blockley*, 1632, Elizabeth, dau. of Sir William Leigh of Longborow, co. Glouc. [He was a loyalist, and during the Great Rebellion was forced to pay £1246 composition for his estates, which had been sequestered. (Atkyns.) His will was proved at Gloucester. His monument in the church at Stow bears a long Latin inscription. (Bigland.)]

Daughters:
 i ELIZABETH,[4] wife of William Brangman, after mar. to John Sanders, a Captain in Her Majesty's Foot Guards. [In 1676 she was "Elizabeth Saunders, widow."]
 ii GRACE[4])
 iii GRACE[4] } all died young.
 iv ISABELLA[4])
Sons (order uncertain):
6 i JOHN[4] [b. about 1643].
 ii WILLIAM.[4])
 iii GILES[4] } died young.
 iv STRANGEWAYS[4] [An abstract of his will is given below].)
 v THOMAS,[4] living unmar. 1683.
 vi EDMUND[4] Chamberlaine of Churchdown, co. Glouc., m. Elizabeth, dau. of Thomas Yate of Glouc.

5 EDMUND[3] CHAMBERLAINE [*Thomas[1] Edmund[2]*] of Maugersbury, ob. 1676, æt. 65; m. Eleanor, dau. of Humphry Colles of Clatterslad, co. Glouc., *bap. at Sevenhampton*, 1616. [April 12, 1634, his father settled upon him an estate, described in 1631 as "one messuage and 4 virgates of land there in the tenure of *John Hannes*, one messuage and 2 virgates of land there in the tenure of *Robert Keble*, and ½ a virgate of land there in the tenure of *Ralph Longworth*; all which premises . . . were lately parcel of the said manor of Malgersbury," and in 1634 as "3 messuages and 6½ virgates of land,"—that is, three home-

CHAMBERLAINE OF MAUGERSBURY 75

steads and about 200 acres,—"to hold for 80 years, he paying yearly for the same one grain of pepper." His will shows that he died possessed of a valuable estate. See the abstracts from the Prerogative Court of Canterbury given below. His tombstone in the church at Stow reads: "Here lyeth Interred the Body of *Colonel* EDMUND CHAMBERLAYNE, who departed this Life, 11 day of April, 1676." (Bigland.)]

Daughters;
  i GRACE,[4] wife of Robert Mathew of Mass Maur, co. Glamorgan, *bap.* 1638 *at Lower Guiting.*
  ii ELIANOR,[4] wife of John Robbins of Bristol, Barrister at Law, *bap.* 1639 *at Lower Guiting.*
  iii DOROTHY,[4] wife of Edward Ridley, Steward to the Duke of Somerset.
  iv ELIZABETH,[4] wife of Henry Robbins of London.
  v ANNE,[4] d. unmar.
Sons:
  i JOHN,[4] died young.
7 ii EDMUND[4] [b. about 1644.]
  iii HUMPHRY[4] CHAMBERLAINE of Abbots Leigh, co. Somerset; m. Elizabeth, dau. of —— Leicester of London. [In 1676, he had two sons, *Edmund* and *John,* and a daughter *Elynor.*]
  iv THOMAS[4] CHAMBERLAINE of Virginia; m. Mary, dau. of Abraham Wood of Virginia.
  v GILES[4]   } died young.
  vi NICHOLAS[4] }

6 JOHN[4] CHAMBERLAINE [*Thomas,*[1] *Edmund,*[2] *John*[3]] of Maugersbury, Esq., Justice of Peace for the co., living 1683, æt. 40, *died* 1691; m. Mary, dau. of Walter Savage of Broadway, co. Worc., Esq. [She d. Dec. 17, 1689. Their tombstones are in the church at Stow. See below the abstract of his will.]

Children:
  i ELIZABETH,[5] æt. 16 [in 1683].
  ii MARY,[5] æt. 14 [in 1683].
8 iii EDMUND[5] CHAMBERLAINE, eldest son, æt. 13, Oct., 1683.
  iv JOHN,[5] died young.
  v SARAH,[5] æt. 9 [in 1683].

7 EDMUND[4] CHAMBERLAINE [*Thomas,*[1] *Edmund,*[2] *Edmund*[3]] of Maugersbury, living æt. 38, 1683; m. Mary, dau. of Sir John Knight of Temple Street in Bristol. [Their tombstone in the church at Stow reads: "Here lyeth interred the Body of EDMUND CHAMBERLAYNE, *Gent.* eldest surviving Son of *Colonel* EDMUND CHAMBERLAYNE, who departed this Life, 15 day of June, in the Year of our Lord God 1696, his Age was 52 Years and three Months. Here also lies the Body of MARY, Widow of the said EDMUND CHAMBERLAYNE, and one of the Daughters of *Sir* JOHN KNIGHT, of *Southmead* in the County of *Gloucester, Knt.,* who died the 26th day of Nov., 1732, Anno æt. 86." (Bigland.)]

Children:
  i Martha[5]
  ii Eleanor[5]
  iii Anne[5]   } all died young.
  iv Mary[5]
  v Edmund[5]
  vi John,[5] only child, living 1683, æt. 1 year.

8 EDMUND[5] CHAMBERLAINE [*Thomas,*[1] *Edmund,*[2] *John,*[3] *John*[4]] æt. 13, Oct., 1683, ob. 1755, æt. 84, C. P. C.; m. *Emma, dau. of James, Lord Chandos,* ob. 1738. [He was married at Westminster Abbey May 26, 1692, to Emma Bridges, daughter of James, eighth Lord Chandos, by Elizabeth, eldest daughter and coheir of Sir Henry Bernard of London, kt. (J. L. Chester, *Marriage, Baptismal and Burial Registers of*——— *Westminster Abbey,* p. 32.) Their tombstone, in the church at Stow, reads: "H. S. E. *The Honble.* Emma Chamberlayne, who departed this Life, the 19 day of June, 1738, Aged 77 Years. Edmund Chamberlayne, Esqr., her Husband, who died 11 day of Febr., 1765 [1755], Aged 84 Years." (Bigland.) He was high-sheriff of Gloucestershire in 1705. He held "a courtleet in this parish [Stow], and divers other adjoining parishes," among them Church-Down, where he was lord of the manor, as at Stow and Maugersbury. (Atkyns.)]

Sons:
  i *John,*[6] eldest son, b. 1693, ob. *col.* 1714.
  ii *Edmund*[6] *Chamberlayne, only surviving son, ob.* 1774. *C. P. C.* m. *Elizabeth, dau. and coheir of Robert Atkins of Nether Swell, co. Glouc.,* mar. 1728, *at Lower Guiting.* [According to this pedigree as continued by Sir Thomas Phillipps, he had eight children. His eldest son, James Montagu[7] Chamberlayne, dying in 1754, his second son, Rev. John[7] Chamberlayne, Rector of Little Ilford, Essex, became heir to the estates. The direct male line ended with the latter's son, Edmund John[8] Chamberlayne, who died without issue in 1831, but the manor-house is still owned by a descendant of Sir Thomas Chamberlayne, who has assumed the name of Chamberlayne.]

ABSTRACTS FROM THE PREROGATIVE COURT OF CANTERBURY

Edmund Chamberlayne 27 January, 1675. I, Edmund Chamberlayne of Malgersbury in Co. Gloucester, Esqr.

I give all my messuages, lands, tenements and hereditaments in Stow-on-the Wold, Malgersbury and Nether-swell in Co. Gloucester to my son Edmund Chamberlaine for 99 years; after that term, to my Kinsman Thomas Chamberlayne of Waringde, in the parish of Wanburrow, in Co. Wilts, Esqr., and to Edmond Webbe of Radborne in the said county, Esq., and their heirs, for the life of my said son Edmond, he to have all the rents thereof for his life; after his decease, his first and every other son and their heirs male to have the said rents; for default, if the said Edmund die leaving his wife with child, then I leave all the said premises to his said wife until the child be born; if it be a son, then I leave to him all the said premises and to the heirs male of his body; for default, I give the same to my son Humfery Chamberlayne for 99 years; after that term, to the said Thomas Chamberlayne and Edmund Webb and their heirs for the life of my said son Humfery, he to take the profits thereof for life; after his decease, I give the same to the first and other sons of the said Humfery and their heirs male, with like proviso as to child unborn: for default, I give the same to my son Thomas Chamberlaine for 99 years, with remainders and proviso as above; for default, I give the same to my son Giles Chamberlayne for 99 years, with like remainders and proviso; and for default, to my right heirs forever.

Whereas, I have at present a sum of money in the hands of William Stratford of Wick Risington, in Co. Gloucester, Esq., secured to be paid to me by a mortgage of the lands of the said William, lying in Wick Risington; I now give the said money to the said Thomas Chamberlayne and Edmund Webb, Esqs., to purchase land of a good title, and cause it to be assured to my posterity in like manner as the lands abovesaid.

My son Edmund shall have all my lands, etc., in Malgersbury which I hold by lease, for his life; at his decease his issue male to have them for residue of said leases; for default, my son Humfery to have them for life and then his issue male; for default, my son Thomas to have the same for his life, and then his issue male; for default, then my said Giles to have the same as above; for default, I give the same to the executors of my son Edmund for ever.

To my daughter Dorothy, £1,000. To my daughter Elizabeth, £800; also £200 which I lent to William Dalton, Esq.

To my son Thomas, £200. To my son Giles, a rent charge of £40 per annum, issuing out of the lands formerly of Ralph Garners and Thomas Haddons in Malgersbury. To my son Humfery, all my lands, etc., in Abbotts Leigh in Co. Somerset for residue of my terms therein; after his decease, I give the residue of said terms to Edmund Chamberlayne, eldest son of the said Humfery; after his decease, to John, second son of the said Humfery.

To the said trustees I give £200, to employ the interest thereof for the benefit of my daughter Grace the now wife of Robert Mathews, Esq., for her life; after her death the said money to be paid to Grace, Thomas, Mary, and Robert Mathews, children of the said Robert and Grace, at their ages of 21. To my said daughter Dorothy all my gold money and my best piece of plate, etc. To my grandchildren Elynor and John Chamberlayne, children of my son Humfery, £100 each, at their ages of 21. To my niece Mrs. Susan White, £100, and £5 for mourning. To each of the other children of my deceased sister Mrs. Grace White, £5.

All my children who shall be unmarried at my death, and willing to continue in the house where I shall die, shall have 'diett and other necessary entertainement' there at the charge of my executors for six months after my death.

To the poor of Stow £5, and to the poor of Malgerbury 40s. to be disposed of by my neighbour Robert Kible. To my servant Joan Hill, £10.

The rest of my goods to my said son Edmund whom I make executor. The said Thos. Chamberlayne and Edmund Webb to be overseers.

Witnesses: Rich: Hayward, Francis Dix, Senior and Francis Dix, Junior. Proved 9 June, 1676, by the executor.—61 Bence.

STRANGWAYES CHAMBERLAYNE. 2 January 1676. I, Strangwayes Chamberlayne of London, merchant.

To my sister Elizabeth Saunders, widow, £100, desiring my brother Thomas Chamberlayne to pay the same out of the money remaining in his hands. To my brother John Chamberlayne, £10. To my brother Edmund Chamberlayne £10. I order £80 to be laid out for my funeral expenses. To Samuel Powell £5 and I make him overseer. To Elizabeth Mitchell £5. I make my said sister Elizabeth Saunders sole executrix.

The mark of the said Strangwayes Chamberlayne.

Witnesses: James Fletcher, B. D., Nathaniel Unwin.

Proved 9 January 1676, by the executrix.—4 Hale.

GILES CHAMBERLAINE. On 25 June 1681, commission to Bernard Dutton, principal creditor of Giles Chamberlaine, late of Stow, Co. Gloucester, but who died at Tangier, in parts beyond the seas, bachelor, to administer the goods, etc.— Admon. Act Book, 1681."

THOMAS CHAMBERLAYNE. 9 May 1687. I, Thomas Chamberlayne of Oddington in Co. Gloucester, Esq.

To the poor of Oddington 40s. and to the poor of Stow in Co. Gloucester £5, and to the poor of Over Norton in Co. Oxford £3.

To my son Thomas Chamberlaine 40s., to his wife 20s. and to his two children 10s. each. To my daughter Christian Gibbs 20s., she having had a portion already, and to her five children 10s. each. To Katherine Chamberlayne, youngest daughter of my son John, deceased, £200. To my daughter Katherine Hearst, 20s., she having had a portion already. To my daughter Margaret Danvers, 20s. only, for like reason, and to her husband 20s. To my daughter Elizabeth £600. To my daughter Anne £600. I give my son Robert Chamberlayne all the money he owes me.

I make my son-in-law, Mr. Anthony Gibbs, Mr. Edward Hearst, and my grandson Charles Gibbs executors: if any of them die I appoint my cousin Edmond Chamberlayne of "Maugresbury" executor.

To my daughter Grace £500 which my son Thomas is to pay to my executors, and which is secured by certain lands in Oddington.

I give to my executors the lands and tenements which I hold of Brazenose College in Oxford called the Pryory in Co. Oxford, to sell the same to pay my debts, etc.

Witnesses: ———— Pissbery, Thomas Phipps, Amy Paine.

Proved 7 June 1689, by the said Charles Gibbs.—76 Ent.

JOHN CHAMBERLAINE. 27 February 1691. I, John Chamberlaine of Maugesbury in Co. Gloucester, Esq.

My son Edmond Chamberlayne of the Inner Temple, London, gentleman, to be executor, and I give him all my goods. To George Townesend of Lincoln's Inn, gentleman, 20 guineas.

Witnesses: Tho: Compere, Edward Freeman.

Proved 6 July 1692, by the executor.—125 Fane.

EDMUND CHAMBERLAYNE. 23 January 1696-97, commission to Mary Chamberlayne, relict of Edmund Chamberlayne, late of Maugesbury, in the parish of Stow-on-the-Wold, in Co. Gloucester to administer, etc.—Admon. Act Book, 1697.

These abstracts were ordered from England by Mr. George W. Chamberlain for Rev. Leander T. Chamberlain, D.D., when Chairman of the Committee on English Ancestry, and were calendared in the Report of the Chamberlain Association for 1902. They are printed from copies furnished at the request of the Committee on Publication.

ANCESTRY OF SIR THOMAS CHAMBERLAIN OF PRESTBURY

BY SIR ROBERT ATKYNS (1647-1711) OF GLOUCESTERSHIRE

"This ancient family of the Chamberlains is descended from John [William?] count de Tankervile, of Tankervile castle in Normandy, who came into England with king William the Conqueror, but returned again into Normandy. John de Tankervile was a younger son of the former earl, and was lord chamberlain to king Henry the First. Richard Chambelain, son of the last John, was lord chamberlain to king Stephen, and thereupon assumed the surname of Chamberlain ['and gave for Arms 1 & 4. Gules, an Inescutcheon, Argent, in an Orle of eight Mullets, Or: 2 and three Gules, a Chevron, between three Escallops, Or, which his descendants bear at this day.' (Wotton, 1741.) The quartering seems to date from 1174. See below]. He married the daughter of Galfrey ————. William Chamberlain, lord of North Riston, was son of Richard; he also was lord chamberlain to king Henry the Second, and married the daughter of Clifton; he had taken prisoner Robert de Bellemont, earl of Millain in Normandy, and earl of Leicester in England, commonly called Blanchmaines, who had taken part with young king Henry against the king his father; and for this service the king granted him to quarter the arms of the earl of Leicester with the arms of Tankervile, in the year 1174. Robert Chamberlain was son of William. Sir Richard Chamberlain was son of Robert; he married Jane daughter and heir of John Gatesden. Sir Robert Chamberlain, son of sir Richard, married the daughter of Griffeth of Northamptonshire. Sir John Chamberlain was son of sir Robert; he married Jane, daughter and heir of John Mortein [son of Sir John Mortein, and grandson of Sir Nicholas

Mortein] descended from an ancient family of that name, and whose mother was daughter and heir of [Richard] Ekney [of Ekney in Buckinghamshire]. Sir Richard Chamberlain, son of sir John, married Jane daughter of sir John Reins, of Clifton Reins [in Buckinghamshire. She died 11 Henry IV].

"Sir Richard Chamberlain, eldest son of sir Richard, was settled at Sherborne in Oxford-shire: his posterity continued there until John Chamberlain, the last of that branch, died in the reign of king James the First, and left two daughters coheiresses: the elder daughter was first married to sir Thomas Gage [of Firle, in Sussex, Bart.] and afterwards to sir William Goring of [Burton] Sussex; the younger daughter was married to the lord Abergavenny. ['Francis Chamberlayne, Esq., late Member of Parliament for New-Shoreham, and Richard Chamberlayne, Esq., of Princethorpe, in Com. Warwick, were descended from this branch of the Chamberlaynes. Which Richard Chamberlayne, Esq., was late High-Sheriff of the county of Essex, and married Sarah, daughter and heir of Jeffery Stanes, Esq., of Ryes in Essex, by whom he has only one Son, Stanes Chamberlayne.' Wotton, 1741.]

"John Chamberlain, of Hopton in Derbyshire, [Esq.] was second son of sir Richard the elder, and brother to sir Richard Chamberlain the younger: he married [Alice] the daughter of Bensted. Thomas Chamberlain was son of John: he married Isabel the daughter of Knifton. John Chamberlain, son of Thomas, married the daughter of Elton. John Chamberlain, son of John, married Agnes the daughter of Keynes [Reynes?]. William Chamberlain, son of the last John, married Elizabeth, daughter of Fleming of Dartmouth.

"Sir Thomas Chamberlain of Presbury, son of William, married Anne Vander-Zenny, of the house of Nassaw of the Low Countries: his second wife was Elizabeth daughter of sir John Luddington, and widow of ——— Machine, from whom are descended the Chamberlains of Maugersbury ['whose heir-general is Edmund Chamberlayne, Esq. Of this family is also the Reverend Thomas Chamberlayne, D. D., Dean of Bristol, and Chaplain in ordinary to his Majesty.' Wotton, 1741]. His third wife was Anne, daughter of Kirkeet, and [half] sister of sir ——— Monke of Devonshire, grandfather to the duke of Albermarle, from whom are descended the Chamberlains of Oddington ['which said family is lately extinct.' Wotton, 1741]. This sir Thomas was eminent for his publick services: he was ambassador in the reigns of king Henry the Eighth, king Edward the Sixth, and queen Elizabeth. ['A younger brother to this Sir Thomas Chamberlayne, was William Chamberlayne, Esq., who settled in Ireland, and left one son Thomas; who applying himself to the study of the laws of England, and being eminent in his profession, was first knighted by King James I, and soon after advanced by him to be Chief Justice of Chester.' (Wotton.) His biography is given in the *Dictionary of National Biography*, edited by Sidney Lee. He died in 1625, leaving two sons. The younger, George Chamberlayne, Esq., of Wardington, Oxfordshire, 'married Anne daughter of Sir Richard Saltinstall, of South Okingdon, in Essex, Knt., and left issue; from whom is descended the present George Chamberlayne, of Wardington, Esq., Member of Parliament for Buckingham, who married a daughter of Sir Thomas Hardy, Knt.' (Wotton, 1741.) Thomas Chamberlayne of Wickham, in Oxfordshire, eldest son and heir of the Chief-Justice of Chester, 'in consideration of his distinguished loyalty to his Majesty, in the time of the great rebellion, and of his ancient descent,' was created a Baronet by King Charles I, February 4, 1642. Sir James Chamberlayne, 'captain in the Royal Regiment of horse-guards, commonly call'd the blue guards,' was Baronet when Wotton wrote in 1741.]

AUTHORITIES

Sir Robert Atkyns, *The Ancient and Present State of Gloucestershire*, p. 365.
Thomas Wotton, *The English Baronetage*, ed. 1741, vol. 2, pp. 374–378.
The Visitation of Oxfordshire in 1566 and 1574, printed in the Publications of the Harleian Society, vol. 5, pp. 235–237.

OFFICERS

President

MAJ.-GEN. JOSHUA L. CHAMBERLAIN, LL.D., Brunswick, Me.

Vice-Presidents

BRIG.-GEN. SAMUEL E. CHAMBERLAIN, Barre, Mass.
COL. THOMAS CHAMBERLIN, Philadelphia, Pa.
REV. ELNATHAN E. STRONG, D.D., Boston, Mass.
PROF. THOMAS C. CHAMBERLIN, LL.D., Chicago, Ill.
MYRON L. CHAMBERLAIN, M.D., Boston, Mass.
COL. SIMON E. CHAMBERLIN, Washington, D. C.
GEORGE M. CHAMBERLIN, M.D., Chicago, Ill.
PRES. MCKENDREE H. CHAMBERLIN, LL.D., Lebanon, Ill.
MR. LEWIS H. CHAMBERLAIN, Detroit, Mich.
GOV. GEORGE E. CHAMBERLAIN, Portland, Oregon.
REV. LEANDER T. CHAMBERLAIN, D.D., New York City.
MR. RICHARD H. CHAMBERLAIN, Oakland, Cal.
MR. WILLIAM WILSON CHAMBERLAINE, Norfolk, Va.
PROF. PAUL M. CHAMBERLAIN, Chicago, Ill.
MR. EMERSON CHAMBERLIN, New York City.
MR. PIERSON M. CHAMBERLAIN, New Jersey.

Corresponding Secretary

MISS ABBIE MELLEN CHAMBERLAIN, 6 Exeter Park, Cambridge, Mass., and Washington, D. C.

Recording Secretary

MR. MONTAGUE CHAMBERLAIN, 35 Congress Street, Boston, Mass.

Treasurer

MR. THOMAS CHAMBERLAIN, State National Bank, Boston, Mass.

Assistant Treasurer

MRS. SOPHIA A. C. CASWELL, 27 River Street, Cambridge, Mass.

Executive Committee

HON. LOYED E. CHAMBERLAIN, *Chairman*, Brockton, Mass.
JUDGE WM. T. FORBES, Worcester, Mass.
MISS LAURA B. CHAMBERLAIN, Cambridge, Mass.
The President, Secretaries, and Treasurers, *ex-officio*.

STANDING COMMITTEES

Genealogical Committee

COL. WILLIAM T. HARDING, *Chairman*, 146 Broadway, New York City.
COL. THOMAS CHAMBERLIN, Philadelphia, Pa.
MR. HERBERT B. CHAMBERLAIN, Brattleboro, Vt.
GEORGE M. CHAMBERLIN, M.D., Chicago, Ill.
MISS JENNIE CHAMBERLAIN WATTS, Cambridge, Mass.
MR. GEORGE R. CHAMBERLAIN, New Haven, Conn.
REV. A. J. FRETZ, Milton, N. J.

Committee on English Ancestry

MR. SAMUEL D. CHAMBERLIN, Hartford, Conn.
MR. ROSWELL W. CHAMBERLAIN, Chester, N. Y.
MRS. HARRIET P. KIMBALL, Dubuque, Iowa.
MR. CHARLES N. FESSENDEN, Chicago, Ill.
MR. HENRY R. CHAMBERLAIN, London, England.
MRS. CHARLES B. PLATT, Englewood, N. J.
MR. WILLIAM C. CHAMBERLAIN, Dubuque, Iowa.

Committee on History

MAJ.-GEN. JOSHUA L. CHAMBERLAIN, *Chairman*, Portland, Me.
HON. ABIRAM CHAMBERLAIN, Meriden, Conn.
COM. EUGENE T. CHAMBERLAIN, Commissioner of Navigation, Washington, D. C.
MR. MONTAGUE CHAMBERLAIN, Boston, Mass.
MISS LAURA B. CHAMBERLAIN, Cambridge, Mass.
MISS S. EMMA CHAMBERLIN, Cleveland, Ohio.
PROF. RALPH CURTIS RINGWALT, New York City.

Committee on Colonial and American Revolutionary Ancestry

J. W. CHAMBERLIN, M.D., *Chairman*, Endicott Building, St. Paul, Minn.
MR. WM. S. BOYNTON, St. Johnsbury, Vt.
MRS. O. A. FURST, Bellefonte, Pa.
MRS. FLORENCE C. MOSELEY, New Haven, Conn.
MR. PRESCOTT CHAMBERLAIN, Boston, Mass.
MISS ISABELLA S. CHAMBERLIN, Washington, D. C.

Committee on Recent Wars

CAPT. ORVILLE T. CHAMBERLAIN, *Chairman*, Elkhart, Ind.
BRIG.-GEN. SAMUEL E. CHAMBERLAIN, Barre, Mass.
MR. ROLLIN S. CHAMBERLAIN, Wilkesbarre, Pa.
CAPT. HIRAM S. CHAMBERLAIN, Chattanooga, Tenn.
MRS. EMILY A. CAPRON, Winchendon, Mass.
MISS HELEN C. CHAMBERLAIN, Washington, D. C.
MRS. ELLEN E. C. BLAIR, Dorchester, Mass.
MISS S. EMMA CHAMBERLIN, Cleveland, Ohio.

LIST OF MEMBERS

Life Members

Mrs. Lucy P. Chamberlain	Medford, Mass.
†Rev. Leander T. Chamberlain, D.D	New York, N. Y.
Mr. William Chamberlain	West Chesterfield, N. H.
George M. Chamberlin, M. D.	Chicago, Ill.
Rev. Jacob Chamberlain, LL.D	Madras, India
Mr. Charles Willis Smith	Pittsburg, Pa.

Active Members

Mr. Andrew Adams	Kahuku, Oahu, Hawaii
Mrs. George W. Adams	Dorchester, Mass.
*Col. Henry H. Adams (died June 25, 1905)	New York, N. Y.
Mrs. Horace G. Allen	Boston, Mass.
Capt. Abram P. Andrew	La Porte, Ind.
Mrs. Martha E. Austin	Roxbury, Mass.
Mrs. Emily S. Bartlett	Chicago, Ill.
†Mrs. Ellen E. C. Blair	Dorchester, Mass.
Miss Amy E. Blanchard	Philadelphia, Pa.
*Mr. D. C. Bloomer (died February 26, 1900)	Council Bluffs, Iowa.
Mrs. Sarah M. C. Bodwell	Clifton Springs, N. Y.
†Mr. William S. Boynton	St. Johnsbury, Vt.
†Mrs. J. M. Brant	East Weymouth, Mass.
Mrs. George M. Brown	Hartford, Conn.
Mrs. J. S. Brown	La Grange, Ind.
Mrs. Carrie M. Butts	Newton Centre, Mass.
Mrs. Emily A. Capron	Winchendon, Mass.
Mrs. Emma A. Carr	Dorchester, Mass.
†Mrs. Sophia A. C. Caswell	Cambridge, Mass.
†Miss Abbie M. Chamberlain	Cambridge, Mass.
Hon. Abiram Chamberlain	Meriden, Conn.
Mr. Albert Chamberlin	North Abington, Mass.
Mr. Albert S. Chamberlin	Hartford, Conn.
†Mr. A. C. Allen Chamberlain	Winchester, Mass.
Mr. Allen Chamberlin	New York, N. Y.
Mr. Allen G. Chamberlain	Fairbury, Neb.
*Mr. Almond W. Chamberlain (died January 30, 1905)	Harbor Beach, Mich.
Miss Anna P. Chamberlain	East Orange, N. J.
Mr. Archie S. Chamberlain	Paterson, N. J.
Mr. Arthur B. Chamberlain	Rochester, N. Y.
Mr. Arthur Hale Chamberlain	Plainfield, N. J.
†Mr. Asa W. Chamberlin	Jamaica Plain, Mass.
Miss Catherine J. Chamberlayne	Boston, Mass.
Mr. Cecil C. Chamberlain	Enderlin, N. Dak.

* Deceased.
† Charter Members.

LIST OF MEMBERS 85

Mr. Charles A. Chamberlin	Detroit, Mich.
Mr. Charles A. Chamberlain	Forge Village, Mass.
Mr. Charles E. Chamberlin	Roxbury, Mass.
Mr. Charles E. Chamberlain	New Bedford, Mass.
Mr. Charles H. Chamberlin	Kingston, Pa.
*Mr. Charles K. Chamberlin (died May 14, 1899)	Pittsburg, Pa.
Mr. Charles T. Chamberlain	Minneapolis, Minn.
Mr. Charles W. Chamberlain	Dayton, Ohio.
Mr. Charles W. Chamberlain	Seattle, Wash.
Mr. Chauncy W. Chamberlain	Boston, Mass.
Mr. Clarence Abner Chamberlin	Eau Claire, Wis.
Mr. Clarence M. Chamberlain	Rochester, N. Y.
Miss Clarissa A. Chamberlin	West Concord, N. H.
Mr. Curtis A. Chamberlin	Concord, N. H.
*†Cyrus N. Chamberlain, M.D. (died July 18, 1899)	Andover, Mass.
*†Hon. Daniel H. Chamberlain, LL.D. (died April 13, 1907)	W. Brookfield, Mass.
*†Hon. Daniel U. Chamberlin (died June 15, 1898)	Cambridgeport, Mass.
Mr. Davis S. Chamberlain	Des Moines, Iowa
Miss Delia Cara Chamberlin	Burlington, Iowa
*Mr. Dwight S. Chamberlain (died May 11, 1903)	Lyons, N. Y.
Miss Edna W. Chamberlin	Summit, N. J.
Mr. Edward Wilmot Chamberlain, LL.B	New York, N. Y.
*†Mr. Edward Watts Chamberlain (died December 18, 1905)	Louisville, Ky.
Mr. Edward W. Chamberlin	Braintree, Mass.
Mr. Edwin Chamberlain	San Antonio, Tex.
Mr. Edwin Abiel Chamberlin	Spencer, Ind.
Mr. Edward F. Chamberlin	Scranton, Pa.
Mr. Eli H. Chamberlain	Pontiac, Mich.
Miss Elizabeth B. Chamberlin	Chicago, Ill.
Miss Elizabeth E. Chamberlain	Roxbury, Mass.
†Miss Ella J. Chamberlain	Cambridge, Mass.
Miss Ellen Jeanette Chamberlin	Seattle, Wash.
Mr. Emerson Chamberlin	Summit, N. J.
Mr. Ephraim Chamberlain	Norwood, Mass.
Mr. Erastus H. Chamberlin	Detroit, Mich.
Mr. Ernest V. Chamberlin	Camden, N. J.
Mr. Eugene Chamberlin	Brooklyn, N. Y.
*Mr. Eugene G. Chamberlin (died September 1, 1905)	Chicago, Ill.
Hon. Eugene Tyler Chamberlain	Washington, D. C.
Gen. Frank Chamberlain	Albany, N. Y.
Mr. Frank D. Chamberlin	Hartford, Conn.
Mr. Frank E. Chamberlain	Manistee, Mich.
Mr. Frank H. Chamberlin	Hudson, Mass.
Mr. Fred D. Chamberlin	Portland, Ore.
Mr. Fred W. Chamberlin	Detroit, Mich.
Mr. Frederick E. Chamberlin	Bayonne, N. J.
Mr. Frederic W. Chamberlain	Three Oaks, Mich.
Mr. George B. Chamberlin	Chicago, Ill.
Mr. George A. Chamberlin	Yonkers, N. Y.
Mr. George Clinton Chamberlin	Indianapolis, Ind.
George E. Chamberlain, M.D.	Manilla, P. I.
Hon. George E. Chamberlin	Portland, Ore.

CHAMBERLAIN ASSOCIATION OF AMERICA

Mr. George F. Chamberlin	New York, N. Y.
Mr. G. Howard Chamberlin	Yonkers, N. Y.
George M. Chamberlin, M. D.	Chicago, Ill.
Mr. George R. Chamberlain	New Haven, Conn.
Mr. George Thomas Chamberlain	Columbus, Ohio
Mr. George W. Chamberlin	Summit, N. J.
*Rev. George W. Chamberlain, D. D. (died July 31, 1902)	Bahia, Brazil, S. A.
†Mr. George W. Chamberlain	Malden, Mass.
Miss Gertrude Chamberlin	Boston, Mass.
Mr. Harlow H. Chamberlain	Minneapolis, Minn.
Mr. Harold Wyllys Chamberlain	Brunswick, Me.
Mr. Harry G. Chamberlin	Chicago, Ill.
Miss Hattie J. Chamberlain	New Haven, Conn.
Miss Helen Chamberlain	Hyde Park, Mass.
Miss Helen M. C. Chamberlin	Washington, D. C.
*Miss Henrietta M. Chamberlaine (died December 13, 1906)	Baltimore, Md.
*Mr. Henry Chamberlain (died Feb. 9, 1907)	Three Oaks, Mich.
Mr. Henry E. Chamberlin	Gridley, Kan.
Mr. Henry L. Chamberlin	Buffalo, N. Y.
Mr. Henry N. Chamberlain	Chicago, Ill.
Mr. Henry R. Chamberlain	London, Eng.
†Mr. Herbert B. Chamberlain	Brattleboro, Vt.
Capt. Hiram S. Chamberlain	Chattanooga, Tenn.
Mr. Horace A. Chamberlin	Somerville, Mass.
Mr. Horace P. Chamberlain	Buffalo, N. Y.
Mr. Ira Chamberlain	Paterson, N. J.
*Mr. Isaac W. Chamberlin (died December 15, 1904)	Lafayette, Ind.
Mr. Isaac C. Chamberlain	Dubuque, Iowa
Miss Isabella S. Chamberlin	Washington, D. C.
*Mr. Jacob A. Chamberlain (died June 28, 1907)	Warwick, N. Y.
*†Mr. Jacob Chester Chamberlain (died July 28, 1905)	New York, N. Y.
Rev. James A. Chamberlin, D.D.	Berkeley, Cal.
*Mr. James I. Chamberlain (died June 1, 1906)	Harrisburg, Pa.
James P. Chamberlin, M. D.	Boston, Mass.
Mr. James Roswell Chamberlin	Rochester, N. Y.
Mr. James W. Chamberlain	Akron, Ohio
†Miss Jessie C. Chamberlin	Waco, Texas
Mr. John Chamberlin	Lexington, Mo.
*Mr. John F. Chamberlin (died September 14, 1905)	Summit, N. J.
Mr. John W. Chamberlain	Portland, Ore.
*Mr. John Wilson Chamberlin (died August 11, 1901)	Tiffin, Ohio
*Joseph E. M. Chamberlaine, M. D. (died January 30, 1901)	Easton, Md.
Joseph E. Chamberlin	New York, N. Y.
Mrs. Joseph F. Chamberlain	Boston, Mass.
*Mr. Joseph L. Chamberlain (died December 30, 1900)	Cherry Valley, N. Y.
†Maj.-Gen. Joshua L. Chamberlain, LL.D.	Brunswick, Me.
Mr. J. D. Chamberlin	Toledo, Ohio
Mr. Joseph H. Chamberlin	Chicago, Ill.
James P. Chamberlin, M. D.	Boston, Mass.
Mr. Joseph R. Chamberlain	Raleigh, N. C.
†Jehiel W. Chamberlin, M. D.	St. Paul, Minn.
Miss Kaitryn Chamberlain	Albany, N. Y.

LIST OF MEMBERS

†Miss Laura B. Chamberlain	Cambridge, Mass.
Mr. Lee Chamberlain	Los Angeles, Cal.
Mrs. Lee Chamberlain	Los Angeles, Cal.
Mr. Leon T. Chamberlain	St. Paul, Minn.
Mr. Lewis H. Chamberlin	Detroit, Mich.
†Miss Lizzie F. Chamberlain	Cambridge, Mass.
Hon. Loyed E. Chamberlain	Brockton, Mass.
Miss Margaret E. Chamberlain	New York, N. Y.
Mark Chamberlin, D. D. S.	Cody, Wyo.
*Mark A. Chamberlain, M. D. (died July 3, 1905)	Winthrop, Iowa
Mr. Martin H. Chamberlin	Rutland, Vt.
Pres. McKendree H. Chamberlin, LL.D.	Lebanon, Ill.
*†Hon. Mellen Chamberlain, LL.D. (died June 25, 1900)	Chelsea, Mass.
†Mr. Montague Chamberlain	Boston, Mass.
*Mr. Moses Chamberlin (died July 29, 1902)	Milton, Pa.
†Myron L. Chamberlain, M. D.	Boston, Mass.
Mr. Myla Chamberlin	W. Concord, N. H.
*Mr. Nahum B. Chamberlin (died January 11, 1905)	Jamaica Plain, Mass.
*†Mr. Newell Chamberlain (died February 10, 1905)	Cambridge, Mass.
Mr. Norman A. Chamberlain	Charleston, S. C.
*†Miss N. Augusta Chamberlain (died March 22, 1900)	Auburndale, Mass.
*Rev. Nathan H. Chamberlayne (died April 1, 1901)	Monument Beach, Mass.
*Mr. Orin S. Chamberlain (died February, 1902)	Chicago, Ill.
Capt. Orville T. Chamberlain	Elkhardt, Ind.
Mr. Patrick Chamberlaine	Chicago, Ill.
Prof. Paul Mellen Chamberlain	Chicago, Ill.
Mr. Pierson M. Chamberlain	Netcong, N. J.
Mr. Prescott Chamberlain	Chelsea, Mass.
Mr. Preston S. Chamberlin	Bradford, Vt.
Raymond Chamberlain, Ph.D.	Brooklyn, N. Y.
Mr. Remembrance W. Chamberlain	Bradford, Vt.
Mr. Richard H. Chamberlain	Oakland, Cal.
Gen. Robert H. Chamberlain	Worcester, Mass.
Mr. Robert M. Chamberlain	Detroit, Mich.
Mr. Rollin S. Chamberlin	Harrisburg, Pa.
Mr. Roswell W. Chamberlain	Chester, N. Y.
†Brig.-Gen. Samuel E. Chamberlain	Barre Plains, Mass.
Miss Sarah Abigail Chamberlin	Cumberland Foreside, Me.
†Miss Sarah P. Chamberlain	Salem, Mass.
Mr. Sylvester Chamberlain	Buffalo, N. Y.
†Col. Simon E. Chamberlin	Washington, D. C.
†Miss S. Emma Chamberlin	Cleveland, Ohio
Mr. Samuel D. Chamberlin	Hartford, Conn.
Mr. S. Harrison Chamberlain	Allston, Mass.
Mr. Smith T. Chamberlin	Derby, Conn.
*Mr. Stillman W. Chamberlain (died September 20, 1903)	Braintree, Mass.
Mr. Strond N. Chamberlain	Netcong, N. J.
Mr. Theodore Chamberlain	Hackensack, N. J.
†Prof. Thomas C. Chamberlin, LL.D.	Chicago, Ill.
†Col. Thomas Chamberlin	Philadelphia, Pa.
†Mr. Thomas Chamberlain	Hyde Park, Mass.
Mr. Thomas E. Chamberlin	Brookline, Mass.

Mr. Walter N. Chamberlin..New Carlisle, Ohio
*Mr. Ward B. Chamberlin (died November 14, 1903).............New York, N. Y.
Mr. Warren Chamberlain...Honolulu, H. I.
Mr. Wesley Chamberlain...Newfoundland, N. J.
Capt. Wilbur F. Chamberlain..Hannibal, Mo.
Mr. Willard C. Chamberlin..Newton Centre, Mass.
Mr. Willard DeWitt Chamberlin...Dayton, Ohio
Mr. Willard N. Chamberlain..Brookline, Mass.
Mr. William Chamberlain..Portland, Me.
Mr. William Chamberlain..Ashbourne, Pa.
Capt. William Chamberlaine...Fortress Monroe, Va.
*Prof. William B. Chamberlain (died March 7, 1903)..........Oak Park, Ill.
Mr. William B. Chamberlin..Torresdale, Pa.
Mr. William C. Chamberlain..Charlottesville, Va.
Mr. William C. Chamberlain..Dubuque, Iowa
†Mr. William Carlton Chamberlain......................................Cannelton, Ind.
Mr. William H. Chamberlin..Chicago, Ill.
Mr. William H. Chamberlin..Roxabell, Ohio
Rev. William I. Chamberlain, Ph.D.....................................New Brunswick, N. J.
Mr. William Joseph Chamberlain...Denver, Colo.
*Mr. William N. Chamberlin (died August 9, 1901)............Pittsfield, Mass.
Major William N. Chamberlin...Washington, D. C.
Mr. William Porter Chamberlain...Knoxville, Tenn.
Mr. William R. Chamberlain..Chicago, Ill.
Mr. William Reginald Chamberlain.....................................Portland, Me.
Mr. William S. Chamberlain..Cleveland, Ohio
Mr. William W. Chamberlaine...Norfolk, Va.
*†Mrs. Alice G. Chamberlain Clarke (died July 8, 1899)......Southbridge, Mass.
Mrs. Mary L. C. Clarke...Andover, Mass.
Mrs. Alfred W. Cole...Boston, Mass.
Mrs. George N. Conklin..Marquette, Mich.
†Edward Cowles, M.D., LL.D..Boston, Mass.
Miss Caroline Crosman...Detroit, Mich.
*Mrs. Amie Whiting Damon (died January 26, 1902).........Reading, Mass.
Mrs. Nathan A. Davis...Concord, Mass.
Mrs. Nestor W. Davis...Winchester, Mass.
Mrs. A. E. Dick...Andover, Mass.
Mrs. Nelson R. Doe...Bradford, Vt.
Miss Hattie Chamberlin Drew..Brooklyn, N. Y.
Mr. John C. Eccleston..Lewisburg, Pa.
Mrs. Sarah C. Eccleston...Buenos Ayres, S. A.
Mrs. James A. Eddy..Aspen, Colo.
Mr. Elbert Eli Farman..Warsaw, N. Y.
Mrs. Mary E. Fellows...New York, N. Y.
Mr. Charles N. Fessenden..Chicago, Ill.
Judge William T. Forbes..Worcester, Mass.
Miss Harriott A. Fox..Chicago, Ill.
Miss Mary Headley Fretz...Milton, N. J.
†Mrs. Caroline W. Furst..Bellefonte, Pa.
Miss Adelaide C. Gray..Lynn, Mass.
Miss Mary E. Grover...White River Junction, Vt.
†Mrs. Helen Guilford..Minneapolis, Minn.

LIST OF MEMBERS

*Mrs. O. H. Harding (died January 30, 1903)	Allston, Mass.
Mrs. Wm. J. Harding	Brooklyn, N. Y.
Mrs. George B. Harvey	New York, N. Y.
Mrs. William Hayes	Winona, Minn.
Mr. Benj. F. Henry	Olathe, Kansas
Mrs. Harriet C. L. Hewitt	Saratoga Springs, N. Y.
†Miss Louise H. Hinckley	Cambridge, Mass.
Mrs. Hattie T. C. Hughes	Mobile, Ala.
Mrs. H. D. Hurley	Seattle, Wash.
Mrs. Cleora E. Jefferds	Foxcroft, Me.
*Mr. Charles A. Jewell (died January 25, 1905)	Hartford, Conn.
*Miss Charlotte A. Jewell (died October 23, 1903)	Hartford, Conn.
Mrs. A. E. Johnson	So. Newbury, Vt.
Mrs. Annie B. Chamberlain Keene	Bangor, Me.
†Mrs. Etta F. C. Kendall	Auburndale, Mass.
*†Mrs. Eliza M. C. Kennedy (died September 21, 1903)	Watertown, Mass.
†Mrs. Harriet P. Kimball	Dubuque, Iowa
Mrs. Israel H. Light	Bloomington, Ill.
Mrs. Helen M. C. Lloyd	Chicago, Ill.
Mrs. Archibald G. Loomis	Providence, R. I.
Mrs. Margaret C. MacFadden	Oak Park, Ill.
Mrs. C. B. McLean	Pittsburg, Pa.
Miss Mamie L. McCormick	Sparta, N. J.
Mr. Robert L. McCormick	Tacoma, Wash.
*Rev. Moses Mellen Martin, D.D. (died September 25, 1902)	Ovid, Mich.
Mrs. James A. Merritt	Baltimore, Md.
Rev. Oscar F. Moore	Jamaica Plain, Mass.
Mrs. Oscar F. Moore	Delhi, Ohio
Mrs. Edwin T. Mander	Elizabeth, N. J.
Mrs. W. E. F. Moore	Summit, N. J.
Mrs. Florence Chamberlain Moseley	New Haven, Conn.
Mrs. M. P. Murray	Athens, Pa.
Mrs. Charles C. Nicholls	St. Louis, Mo.
Mrs. Evan Oldfield	Booneville, N. Y.
*Mr. John Chamberlain Ordway (died April 23, 1905)	Concord, N. H.
Miss Amy Katherine Pearson	Baltimore, Md.
†Mr. George Herbert Perry	Revere, Mass.
†Mrs. Minnie A. C. Perry	Cambridge, Mass.
†Mr. Ralph Dana Perry	Cambridge, Mass.
Mrs. Ralph F. Perry	Watertown, Mass.
Mrs. Charles B. Platt	Englewood, N. J.
Mrs. Arthur H. Pray	Brookline, Mass.
Miss Lucinda C. Ragan	London, Ohio
Mr. Roe Reisinger	Franklin, Pa.
Mr. John S. Ringwalt, Jr.	Mt. Vernon, Ohio
Prof. Ralph Curtis Ringwalt	New York, N. Y.
Mrs. Elisha Risley	West Hartford, Conn.
Mrs. Albert S. Roe	New York, N. Y.
Miss Emma Ten-Broeck Runk	Lambertville, N. J.
†Mrs. Charles W. Seymour	Hingham, Mass.
Mrs. Amy Chamberlain Shanks (died January 23, 1905)	Round Lake, N. Y.
Miss Maria Gove Shanks	Staten Island, N. Y.

CHAMBERLAIN ASSOCIATION OF AMERICA

Mr. Frank C. Shipley . . . . Seattle, Wash.
Mrs. Anna Eugenia Smiley . . . . Holyoke, Mass.
Mrs. Charles Willis Smith . . . . Pittsburg, Pa.
Mrs. Grace Chamberlin Snook . . . . Hartwell, Ohio
Mr. Arthur C. Sprague . . . . Wollaston, Mass.
Mrs. Louisa Steele . . . . Netcong, N. J.
Mrs. Mary Baldwin Stoddard . . . . Lawrence, Long Island, N. Y.
†Rev. Elnathan E. Strong, D.D. . . . . Auburndale, Mass.
Miss Georgiana Viola Wait . . . . Waltham, Mass.
Mr. Edward K. Warren . . . . Three Oaks, Mich.
Mrs. Edward K. Warren . . . . Three Oaks, Mich.
Miss Jennie Chamberlain Watts . . . . Cambridge, Mass.
Mrs. Martha C. Wilson . . . . Hartford, Conn.
Mrs. Clayton Wrighter . . . . Netcong, N. J.

Associate Members

Mr. George M. Brown . . . . Hartford, Conn.
†Mr. George B. Caswell . . . . Cambridge, Mass.
Mrs. William B. Chamberlin . . . . Torresdale, Pa.
Mrs. Anna Garland Chamberlain . . . . Andover, Mass.
†Mrs. Asa W. Chamberlin . . . . Jamaica Plain, Mass.
Mrs. Catherine W. Chamberlain . . . . Cambridge, Mass.
Mrs. Charles E. Chamberlin . . . . Port Washington, Wis.
Mrs. Eugene Chamberlin . . . . Brooklyn, N. Y.
Mrs. Eugene G. Chamberlin . . . . Brunswick, Me.
Mrs. Fannie E. Chamberlin . . . . Philadelphia, Pa.
Mrs. Jacob C. Chamberlain . . . . New York, N. Y.
Mrs. Mary A. Chamberlin . . . . Greenville, N. H.
†Mrs. Newell Chamberlain . . . . Cambridge, Mass.
Mrs. Robert H. Chamberlain . . . . Worcester, Mass.
Mrs. Samuel E. Chamberlain . . . . Barre Plains, Mass.
Mrs. Thomas Chamberlain . . . . Hyde Park, Mass.
Mrs. James I. Chamberlain . . . . Harrisburg, Pa.
Mr. Nathan A. Davis . . . . Concord, Mass.
Col. William J. Harding . . . . Brooklyn, N. Y.
Mrs. Charles A. Jewell . . . . Hartford, Conn.
†Mr. James H. Kendall . . . . Auburndale, Mass.
Hon. Oscar H. Leland . . . . McGregor, Tex.
Mrs. Sarah J. Ordway . . . . Concord, N. H.
*†Mr. Frank W. Perry (died June 20, 1898) . . . . Cambridge, Mass.
Mrs. Willard N. Chamberlain . . . . Brookline, Mass.

www.ingramcontent.com/pod-product-compliance
Lightning Source LLC
Chambersburg PA
CBHW020118170426
43199CB00009B/564